AF518386

The Novels of Amitav Ghosh
Major Themes

The Novels of Amitav Ghosh
Major Themes

Dr. ANJAN KUMAR
Principal
G. R. Patil College, Dombivli (East)
Dist. Thane (Maharashtra)

ADHYAYAN

ADHYAYAN PUBLISHERS & DISTRIBUTORS
New Delhi-110002

Published by
ADHYAYAN PUBLISHERS & DISTRIBUTORS
4378/4B, 105, J.M.D. House, Murari Lal Street
Ansari Road Darya Ganj, New Delhi - 110002
Ph.: 011-23263018, 011-23277156, Fax: 23280028
Email: adhyayanpublishers@yahoo.com

The Novels of Amitav Ghosh
Major Themes

© Author
Edition 2013
ISBN 978-81-8435-380-8

The responsibility for facts stated, opinion expressed or conclusions reached and plagiarism, if any, in this book is entirely that of the author/ editor. The publisher bears no responsibility for them whatsoever.

Printed in India

Published by Harish Chandra Yadav for Adhyayan Publishers & Distributors, Delhi. Laser Typesetting at Jain Computers and Printed at Tarun Offset Printers, Delhi

DEDICATED

To

My Parents

Preface and Acknowledgements

Fiction, having been the most powerful form of literary expression today, has acquired a prestigious position in Indian English Literature. It is generally agreed that the novel is the most acceptable way of expression of experiences and ideas in the context of our time. The Indian Fiction in English has been attracting worldwide attention. One can wonder whether it is a part of the Indian tradition or the European or the English tradition. A thorough analysis can work out the solution to the problems of tradition and modernity.

Amitav Ghosh has left an indelible impression on the extent of novel writings in Indian writing in English. He has dealt with various themes in his novels. Some of the them include - search for identity, traditions versus modernity, contemporary social problems etc. Ghosh attempts to perceive the lives of his contemporaries in lands as diverse as India, Bangladesh, Egypt, England etc. His canvas is often large and his novels are peopled with a variety of characters, though not in the range of a Tolstoy or a Dosteovesky. As a Calcuttan, Ghosh never moves away from Calcutta and the city comes alive on his pages. The streets of Calcutta and the landmarks of this city in some of his novels take us on a guided tour of the city. Characterization is his forte. Every significant character is delineated realistically. As a post-colonial writer, cultural heritage and identity have become important facets of

Ghosh's personality. The keen ability for deep research that is seen in this novel is a quality generally not associated with Indian writers writing in English. History is easily woven into the narrative framework. Ghosh attempts a comparative study of Asian and African, Indian and Egyptian, Jewish and Islamic cultures. Using the autobiographical traveller's tale to study the past, Ghosh's canvas here is vaster than that of his other novels and his brush-strokes wider. Character delineation has been handled expertly by Ghosh in most of his novels and the three dimensional characters - Abu Ali, Musa Mustafa Jabir, Sabry et al - bring life and colour to his fiction.

An humble attempt has been made in this small project to incorporate all the major aspects of author's writing. I express my heart-felt thanks to all those who have directly or indirectly helped me complete this book. At the outset I am very much thankful to the Chairman of Mumbra Shikshan Prasarak Mandal, Mr. G.R. Patil, who have always been a source of inspiration to me in my academic accomplishments and who has ever given me a free hand to work as a principal in his G.R.Patil College of Arts, Science and Commerce, Dombivli (E), Mumbai. Despite my very busy schedule in the college I always considered it my duty, commitment and responsibility to join the discussion and research forum of the scholars and learners who have ever been striving hard to open up new vistas of learning and the outcome is the present work.

I would like to acknowledge the deep sense of my gratitude to my father Dr. L.K..Sahay,, Rtd. Prof. of Geography and my mother who have taught me to work ceaselessly and honestly for the service of the nation and that of the humanity at large.

I am equally grateful to the librarian of Mumbai University, British library in Mumbai and the library of the University Department of English, Mumbai University, Mumbai for their support and help.

Contents

1
Introduction

Indian English Literature or Indian Literature in English has attracted a widespread interest recently both in India and abroad. It has come to occupy a greater significance in world literature. It is now realized that Indian English Literature and Commonwealth Literature are in no way inferior to other literatures. The writers in Australia, New Zealand, West Indies, South Africa, Canada, Nigeria and India have contributed substantially to the modern English literature.

The first Indian English Novel was written by Bankim Chandra Chatterjee, who left it incomplete and switched over to Bengali in his mother tongue. His *Raj Mohan's Wife* is different from his Bengali novels such as *Durgesh Nandani* or *Kapal Kundla*. In fact, his first novel *Raj Mohan's Wife* paved the way for *Anand Math* [1884] India's first political novel which gave the Indians their national anthem 'Bande Matram'. Ramesh Chandra Dutta, another Bengali novelist translated two of his six novels into English: *The Love of Palms* [1902] and *Slave Girl of Agra* [1909]. These novels aimed at the elimination of social evils. None can deny the fact that the roles of the novelists up to 1935 paved the way for successful socially conscious writing as *Coolie* [1936], *Kanthapura* [1938], *Nectar in a Sieve* [1954] and *The Guide* [1958].

Post-independence Indian English fiction retains the momentum, which it had during the Gandhian age. The tradition of social realism established on a sound of footing earlier is still maintained by novelists like Bhabani Bhattacharya, Manohar Malgonkar and Khushwant Singh. The fiction of B. Rajan illustrates the strains of both realism and fantasy notable development is the emergence of an entire school of women novelists. The leading figures among them are Ruth Prawer Jhabvala, Kamla Markandaya Nayantara Sahgal and Anita Desai. By the end of the 'sixties' and in the early 'seventies' newer voices are heard, the most striking of them are Arun Joshi and Chaman Nahal.

The earliest of the social realists of the period is Bhabani Bhattacharya who is strongly influenced by Tagore and Gandhi and in his fictional theory and practice he shows affinity with M. R. Anand. He is convinced that -

> 'a novel must have a social purpose. It must place before the reader something from the society's point of view' [Joshi, Sudhakar: *An Evening with Bhabani:* 1969]

Bhabani Bhattacharya, therefore, deals with the theme of exploitation - political, economic and social. He has to his credit novels like *So Many Hungers* [1947], *Music for Mohini* [1952], *He Who Rides a Tiger* [1952], *A Goddess Named Gold* [1960], *Shadow From Ladakh* [1966] and *A Dream in Hawaii* [1978].

Unlike Bhattacharya Manohar Malgonkar is a realist who believes that art has no purpose to serve except pure entertainment:

> 'I do strive deliberately and hard to tell a story well. I revel in incident ..... I feel a special allegiance to the particular sub caste among those whose caste mark I have affected, the entertainers the tellers of stories'. [Malgaonkar, Manohar: *'Purdah and Castemarks'*: 1964]

The world of Malgaonkar is one in which women seem to be little more than instruments of masculine pleasure. His famous novels are *Distant Drum* [1960], *Combat of Shadows* [1962], *The Princess* [1963], *A Bend in the Ganges* [1964] and *The Devil's Wind* [1972].

Khushwant Singh declares that 'his roots are in the dunghill of a tiny Indian Village' [Singh, Khushwant: '*Address to Expo1967 Auditorium Montreal*, Canada: 1967]. Whatever the measure of truth in this generalization, it is certainly valid in the case of Khushwant Singh. He appears to take a markedly irreverent view of Indian life and character. His two novels *Train to Pakistan* [1956] and *I Shall Not Hear the Nightingale* [1959] illustrate features of his art.

Balchandra Rajan is less social than psychological in his first novel, *The Dark Dancer* [1959]. In this novel, he appears to pose the problem of East-West confrontation in terms of the protagonist's quest for identity. His second novel, *Too Long in the West* [1961] is the story of Nalini, a south Indian girl, who returns from an American University to face the problem of choosing a suitable husband.

The novels of S. N. Ghose [1899 - 1965] are an exciting experiment in the expression of the Indian ethos. The four novels, *And Gazelles Leaping* [1949], *Cradle of the Clouds* [1951], *The Vermilion Boat* [1953] and *The Flame of the Forest* [1955] form a tetralogy knit together by the central figure of the protagonist narrator, about twenty years of whose life and career they cover.

Of the novelists of the late sixties and the seventies, there are two names Arun Joshi [1939] and Chaman Nahal [1927]. Joshi's recurrent theme is alienation in its different aspects. His heroes are intensely self centered persons prone to self pity and escapism. In his four novels, Joshi deals with four facets of the theme of alienation, in relation to self, the society around, the society outside and humanity at large. Chaman Nahal is a novelist of painful

Odysseys presented in different context. He has also four novels to his credit *My True Face* [1973], *Azadi* [1975], *Into Another Dawn* [1977] and *The English Queens* [1879]. Nahal does not appear to bring either a new perspective or a freshness of treatment to his subject.

The women novelists too form a sizable and significant school. R. P. Jhabvala leads this school. Her best work reveals such inwardness in her picture of certain segments of Indian social life that it is difficult not to consider her as an 'insider' who at the same time enjoys the privilege of being an 'outsider'. Her eight novels fall into two distinct part: Comedies of urban middle class Indian life and East-West encounter.

When Jhabvala can be termed an outsider-insider, Kamla Markandaya is an insider-outsider. She is an expatriate, who has been living in England for a number of years. Her fiction offers a greater variety of setting, character and effect. She is able to create living characters in meaningful dilemmas. She is the writer of more than nine novels such *Nectar in a Sieve* [1954], *Some Inner Fury* [1955], *Possession* [1963], *A Silence of Desire* [1960], *A Handful of Rice* [1966], *The Coffer Dams* [1969], *The Nowhere Man* [1972], *Two Virgins* [1973], and *The Golden Honey Comb* [1977] etc.

Nayantara Sahgal [1927] is regarded as an exponent of the political novel, but it appears that politics is only one of her two major concerns. Besides political theme her fiction is also preoccupied with the modern Indian woman's search for sexual freedom and self-realization. She fails to establish a clear relationship between the political turmoil outside and private torment of broken marriages robs most of her novels of a unified effect of her five novels, *A Time to be Happy* [1958], *This Time of Morning* [1968], *Storm in Chandigarh* [1969] are popular.

Anita Desai, in contrast with other women novelists, is more interested in the interior landscape of the mind than in political and social realities. Writing for her,

> 'is an effort to discover and then to underline, and finally to convey the true significance of things' [Desai, Anita: 'Interview with Yasodhara Dalmia': 1979].

According to her, her novels -

> 'deal with what Ortega if Gasset called the terror of facing, single handed, the ferocious assaults of existence'. [*Ibid* : 1979]

Her protagonists are persons who remain always lonely. Aloneness alone is worth treasuring for them. They are mostly women and for them the emotional traumas sometimes lead to violent death in the end.

One of her assets is that she unravels the volitions of sensibility with subtlety and finesse. She is most capable of evoking the changing aspects of Nature matched with human moods, though her easy mastery of the language, use of images and symbols occasionally result in preciously and over writing. In case her fiction deviates from aloneness and turns to alienation as a metaphysical enigma, a day will come when she will achieve an amplified pattern of significant way of exploration of consciousness comparable to Virginia Woolf.

Very few of the women novelists of this period have attempted so far sustained such fiction writing. Santha Rama Rau's *Remember the House* [1956] is a beautiful picture of the East-West encounter. Her another novel, *The Adventures* [1970] fails to rise above the level of superficiality. Nergis Dalal's *Minari* [1967] is an account of high-class life at a hill station. Her *Two Sisters* [1973] is a contrastive study of twins at opposite poles. *The Inner Door* [1976] has the theme of *Guide* motif of enforced sainthood and *The Girls from Overseas* [1979] can be treated as East-West encounter.

With the growing interest in Indian English literature, there was a sudden spurt of fiction during the nineteen seventies. Notable among them are B. K. Karanjia's novel *More of an Indian* [1970] which deals with Parsi life in

Bombay, V. K. Gokak's *Narahari: Prophet of India* [1972], Timeri Murari's *The Marriage* [1972], Saros Cowasjee's *Goodbye to Elsa* [1975], S. S. Dhami's *Maluka* [1978], Raj Gill's *The Rape* [1974] and *The Infidel* [1979] etc.

The Eighties witnessed the emergence of the second generation of Indian English novelists who were born after independence. With Salman Rushdie's *Midnight's Children* [1981] which won the Booker Prize, the Indian English novel found a voice that shook the English literary world -

> 'with its energy, its self-indulgence, irresponsibility, disorder and cockiness' [Makarand Paranjape: 1990: 220]

As Viney Kirpal points out -

> "The average Indian political consciousness had been inadvertently but dramatically awakened by the close brush with totalitarianism. The Emergency had served as a necessary warning to each slumbering Indian to be an effective watchdog lest the past repeat itself". [1990: xxi]

Shackled to history, the Indian English novelist realized the role that the individual had to play in the nation's life. On the verge of losing one's freedom, democracy and right to dignity, the novelist realized his / her commitments to self-assertain and self-expression. Amitav Ghosh, Vikram Seth, Upmanyu Chatterjee, Rohinton Mistry following Rushdie, on the one hand, brought about the relationship of historio-politico-social aspects of the country and the individual's freedom, his / her quest for truth, and on the other hand. Anita Desai, Shashi Deshpande, Nayantara Sahagal and Dina Mehta broke the long silence and lent voice to the Indian Women's plight.

These voices are heard in the corridors of English literature and they have together made Indian sensibilities felt outside India. It is no longer the westerners peep into India, but India revealed as Indians feel and experience it. They no longer are insecure and uncertain but quite confident and assertive, juxtaposing the Indian characters against the white-the one-tie considered superior race. The Partition theme still persisted for some time, but with a new perspective, how it still affects the older as also the younger generation.

The Indian English novelist has skillfully used this technique of bringing together the fragments of tales, division of time and altering the narrative voice. The novel is no longer of one place, one country, one time-span but is a variegated kaleidoscope of everything and anything put together.

Obviously then, the Indian English novel is here to stay. Interestingly, this is in direct contrast to the earlier predictions and fears about an early death for Indian Writing in English. Writing as late as 1976, Uma Parameswaran says:

> "However, unlike other Anglo-colonial literatures, Indo-English literature seems destined to die young. This Cassandrain prognostication about its imminent extinction is based on a realistic appraisal of current political trends and educational statistics, not on baseless pessimism. Indo-English literature has owned its existence to a peculiar concatenation of political circumstances and the political scene today precludes any optimism regarding the continuance of English". [2]

How wrong this prediction has been is very clear from the writings of the last three decades. That the triumvirate has been left far behind is an obvious fact. Novelists writing now are making a conscious effort at carving out their own niche-with a new thrust in theme, structure, language and even their approach to the entire genre of fiction. As G. R. Taneja puts it rather strongly –

> "It [the novel today] is free from the self-consciousness, shallow idealism and sentimentalism that

characterized the work of the older generation of novelists". [1991: 23]

Whether male or female, these writers have an easy inwardness with the English language, which places them above the colonized writers of the earlier decades.

Amitav Ghosh was born in Calcutta in 1956. He was graduated from Delhi University. He published his first novel *The Circle of Reason* in 1986. He belongs to that elite group of Indian writers writing in English, who attended exclusive schools, almost British, in the post-Raj period and are more comfortable with the English language than with any other Indian language. Harish Trivedi considers this group to be the Stephanie school-products of the elitist St. Stephen's of Delhi. Amitav Ghosh brings to the English language an ease of felicity of expression, which endows all his fiction with a quality of its own. Certainly of writers like Ghosh it can be said that -

> "Expression in English can bring a sense of release to the Indian intellectual as he endeavours to express the deepest turns and twists of his own mind .... Whatever its future form, it seems certain that the Indian novel in English will surpass its counterparts in the regional languages". [Dewett, M. E.: 1962: 584]

Mr. Ghosh's novels reflect a historicity, as history is often present in novels. Even his first novel is an extraordinarily accomplished work of fiction as he innovatively and successfully explores new possibilities for the Indian novel in English. His novels reflect the tendencies and concerns of the age. The modern novel, according to Lionel Trilling,

> "is a perpetual quest for reality and is the most effective agent of the moral imagination". [212]

Ghosh attempts to perceive the lives of his contemporaries in lands as diverse as India, Bangladesh, Egypt, England etc. His canvas is often large and his novels are peopled with a variety of characters, though not in the range of a Tolstoy or a Dosteovesky. As a Calcuttan, Ghosh never moves away from Calcutta and the city comes alive on his pages. The streets of Calcutta and the landmarks of this city in some of his novels take us on a guided tour of the city. Characterization is his forte. Every significant character is delineated realistically. No incongruity strikes us in the development of his characters.

Ghosh's use of time deserves special mention. Most of his novels use time in a non-linear manner. The juxtaposing of past and present is further developed by the use of future too in novels like *The Calcutta Chromosome*. Memory is used aesthetically and effectively to relate the past and the present. His novels have constant time and place shifts. The novels take us to different parts of the world - some common locales and some exotic.

Amitav Ghosh's first novel *The Circle of Reason* [1986] places him immediately as a master craftsman in the art of fiction. Hailed as a breakaway from the traditional forms of fiction writing in English, *The Circle of Reason* has been translated into many European languages and has even won the prestigious literary *Prix Medici Estrangerf* for its French version. Even in his first novel, Ghosh introduces weird and bizarre happenings that are repeated and reiterated and become an intrinsic part of a novel like *The Calcutta Chromosome.* Motifs and metaphors are exerted in plenty with the journey motif being the most recurring one. This is not very surprising when we remember that the author himself has travelled form Bengal to Delhi and later to Egypt and England. He is able to tell a story well. *The Circle of Reason* is about an eight year old orphan who lives in Lalpukur in West Bengal but from where he is on the run. Using the motif of the journey, Ghosh has drama, suspense and mystery too. Shyam Asnani describes the novel:

> "It is also an interesting tale of myriad colourful people, of man's relation with the machine, his curse and salvation with science and reason". [141]

In an Antique Land [1993] unfolds Ghosh's research abilities and interest and in anthropology in which subject he has a research degree. As a post-colonial writer, cultural heritage and identity have become important facets of Ghosh's personality. The keen ability for deep research that is seen in this novel is a quality generally not associated with Indian writers writing in English. History is easily woven into the narrative framework. Ghosh attempts a comparative study of Asian and African, Indian and Egyptian, Jewish and Islamic cultures. Using the autobiographical traveller's tale to study the past, Ghosh's canvas here is vaster than that of his other novels and his brush-strokes wider. Character delineation has been handled expertly by Ghosh in most of his novels and the three dimensional characters - Abu Ali, Musa Mustafa Jabir, Sabry et al - bring life and colour to his fiction. Sharmila Guha concludes Ghosh's achievement in this novel:

> "The barriers of nation, country and time dissolve in the consciousness of the author and he reaches a tragic of how unscrupulous political forces continue to suffocate human aspirants". [1996: 186]

The Calcutta Chromosome [1996], sub-titled A Novel of fevers, Delirium and Discovery, is probably Ghosh's most disappointing novel. Set in Calcutta, it begins as a science fiction but too many issues coalesce to make it a confusing kitsch of sorts. The novel traces the adventures of the enigmatic L. Murugan. Time again used as a significant element but the constant time shifts leave the reader repeatedly confused. In short, myth and superstition, science and grandma's tales combine to make the novel an unrealistic work.

The Shadow Lines [1988] is set in the Calcutta of the 1960's and moves with an easy felicity through Calcutta and Dhaka and London. A young unnamed narrator, his hero, Tridib and the narrator's grandmother provide the basic framework on which the novel moves forward. The time span of the novel extends from 1939 to 1979 with 1964 being a very important year for the characters. Memory lives the past to the present and many of the characters live more in the past than in the present. The novel seems to mock even the concept of exclusive national identity and pride. This is so because riots break out simultaneously both at Dhaka and Calcutta and as a result of the same incident. Snapping of cultural bonds becomes a recurring image in this novel. Lines and boundaries are drawn across continents and countries, but what purpose they serve is an unsolved puzzle. Even ideals nurtured by the freedom struggle suddenly seem meaningless because the disrupted subcontinent today refuses to accept the significance of religious tolerance and brotherhood. In fact, the novel obviously suggests the mindlessness of the violence unleashed in both the countries as fallout of the theft of the Prophet's hair. The killing of Tridib corroborates this when he is on an innocent visit to Dhaka along with Tha'mma and May. Girish Karnad wrote about his visit:

> "Past and future meet across religious, political and cultural barriers in a confusion of emotions, ideals, intentions and acts, leading to a shattering climax". [5]

If narrative can be interpreted as characters in conflict. The Shadow Lines exhibits this appropriately and aesthetically. Characters like Tridib are in conflict with life around them and hence prefer to live by themselves and apart from the rest of family. Jethamoshai and his brother are in conflict with each other. Ila is in conflict with herself never allowing the world to see Nick as he really is. Tha'mma too is in conflict with herself and with her family as she is unable to decide where her home really is. These conflicts provide the momentum required to take the story forward. Writing in post-colonial India, Ghosh realizes that politics and literature cannot be kept separated. As David Cook says –

> "The socially conscious writer does not set to work in a vacuum but urges his society from what it is towards what it might be". [3]

The Shadow Lines has received wide acclaim. That it provides possibilities for a variety of interpretations is obvious from the papers that we have received from our contributors. Urbashi Barat believes that the novel can be examined as a version of 'bildungsroman' as such an analysis will underscore the plurality of experience and meaning conveyed by the novel. As a bildungsroman depicts the young and maturing of a sensitive protagonist, the journey towards individual development and social integration cannot be a smooth one. Shadow Lines becomes a metaphor for the shadowy divisions even between people who are actually mirror images of each other. She reaches the conclusion that *The Shadow Lines* is the quintessential bildungsroman.

Ghosh's sweeping historical novel, *The Glass Palace,* begins with a young boy watching the British stormy the Burmese royal fortress in 1885. Eleven-year-old Rajkumar, an impoverished orphan from India, Sneaks into the forbidden place and meets Dolly, a beautiful young court attendant. Amid the Chaos of looting and violence, Dolly's face is permanently etched into Rajkumar's memory. Soon after, Dolly follows the banished king and queen to India, while Rajkumar stays in Burma, making his fortune in the timber industry. The young man is haunted by Dolly until years later, when he meets her again in India.

Thus, *The Glass Palace* traces the story of their love during the tumultuous 20th Century. Ghosh grounds his work in the unassailable march of history and the unpredictable swings of fate, infusing his novel with a sense of the tragic. History is more than a backdrop for the story of Dolly's and Rajkumar's lives; it is a powerful force that constantly threatens and dwarfs each individual in-the novel. All of Ghosh's characters struggle through an almost overwhelming number of turbulent event. British imperialism, depression, world war II, the Japanese invasion of Burma and Malaya, India's struggle for independence, and military rule in Myanmar. As in his previous work, Ghosh interweaves several intricate plot lines that follow the lives of multiple characters. But The Glass Palace is even more ambitious in the territory it attempts to cover; the story of three generations of three families in Burma, Malaya and India.

The present book studies in detail the voices of the protagonists and other important characters in the novels of Amitav Ghosh. **Chapter One** is Introduction. It unfolds the short history of Indian Fiction in English along with its stress on the contribution of Amitav Ghosh to the literary scenario of Indian English Fiction. **Chapter Two** is entitled as *The Circle of Reason.* It is a huge, ambitious novel with a crowd of characters and themes. It begins with the arrival of orphan, Nachiketa Bose. The novel gives every detail of Alu. **Chapter Three** is called as *The Shadow Lines.* The novel is divided into two parts, *'Going Away'* and *'Coming Home.'* The novel beautifully shifts from past to present and from present to past, Ghosh manages in a masterly way time of two kinds, time past: memory and time present: reality. The first section *'Going Away'* means *'going away from self, 'Coming Home'* means *'Coming back in the self'*. **Chapter Four** is termed as *In an Antique Land.* It talks about the generic borderlines between fact, fiction, autobiography, history, anthropology, and travel book. Ghosh maps ethnographic fieldwork undertaken in the Egyptian villages of Lataifa and Nashawy onto his subsequent research into medieval Indian Ocean trade. In so doing he explores the connections and ruptures between two worlds, the medieval and the contemporary. As the book progresses the two seemingly disparate strands of the Egyptian families and village communities with whom Ghosh resides in the early 1980s, and the narrative of his attempts to trace 'the slave of MS. H.6' increasingly dovetail, each narrative helping to shed light on the other.

Chapter Five is entitled as *The Calcutta Chromosome.* It spreads over one century and three continents, and the main characters are an Egyptian data analyst and a malaria obsessed Indian living in New York City. It's part science fiction, part history, part thriller, part detective story. **Chapter Six** is *The Glass Palace.* It is a historical novel that begins with a young boy watching the British stormy the Burmese royal fortress in 1885. Eleven-year-old Rajkumar, an impoverished orphan from India, Sneaks into the forbidden place and meets Dolly, a beautiful young court attendant. Amid the Chaos of looting and violence, Dolly's face is permanently etched into Rajkumar's memory. Soon after, Dolly follows the banished king and queen to India, while Rajkumar stays in Burma, making his fortune in the timber industry. The young man is haunted by Dolly until years later, when he meets her again in India. The last and the **Seventh Chapter** is 'Conclusion'.

WORKS CITED

Joshi, Sudhakar. 'An Evening with Bhabani', *The Sunday Standard,* 27 April, 1969.

Malgaonkar, Manohar. 'Purdah and Castemarks', *The Times Literary Supplement,* 4 June, 1964.

Singh, Khushwant. 'Address to Expo 1967 Auditorium Montreal, Canada, 1967.

Paranjape, Makarand. 'Inside and Outside the Whale: Politics and the New Indian English Novel', ed. Viney Kirpal, *The New Indian Novel in English,* Delhi: Allied Publishers Pvt. Ltd., 1996.

Kirpal, Viney. Ed. *The New Indian Novel in English,* Delhi: Allied Publishers Pvt. Ltd., 1990.

Parameswaran, Uma. *A Study of Representative Indo-English Novelists,* New Delhi: Vikas, 1976.

Taneja, G. R. 'The Novel Today', *World Literature Today,* University of Oklahama, Spring, 1991.

Dewett, M. E. 'Why Writer in English?' *Times Literary Supplement,* 10 August 1962.

Trilling, Lionel. *The Liberal Imagination,* London, 1961.

Asnani, Shyam. *New Dimensions of Indian English Novel,* Delhi: Doaba House, 1987.

Guha, Sharmila. '*The Shadow Lines* and *In An Antique Land*', London, 1996.

Karnad, Girish. *'Worlds within Worlds'*, Book Review of *The Shadow Lines,* Indian Express Magazine, 18 Dec. 1988.

Cook, David, *African Literature : A Critical View,* London: Orient Longman, 1977.

Devy, G. N. *In Another Tongue,* Chennai: Macmillan, 1995.

2

The Circle of Reason

The Circle of Reason [1986] is the most significant novel by Amitav Ghosh. It deals with the modern man's problem of alienation, migration and the existential crisis in life. Divided into three different sections and called Satva: Reason, Rajas: Passion and Tamas: death, the novel symbolically deals with three phases of human life. Satva: symbolizes the search of wisdom, Rajas symbolizes the life of passion and Tamas stands for darkness, and destruction.

The novel is neither a novel of plot, nor a novel of character, but a novel of thought. There is no conventional development of plot or character. Instead of dealing with one particular character, like R. K. Narayan's *The Guide,* a story of Raju or Mulkraj Anand's *Untouchable,* a story of Bakha, this novel is a story of entire humanity. All characters belong to the world. Like Chaucer's *The Canterbury Tales,* the novel describes all characters with visual details and successfully creates a picturesque effect on reader's mind. Though the characters in the novel are not subtle and complex, they are an epitome of human suffering and pain. In the novel, every one has a story to tell-the story of their untold sufferings. The characters in the novel do not fall into the conventional categories of round and flat characters or types and individual characters. They are descriptive characters. Ghosh's power of imagination, and his keen sense of observation are beautifully revealed in his art of characterization. Here, we have a doctor, a professor, a scientist, a salesman, weavers, a merchant, a lawyer and housewives. Like Chaucer's *The Canterbury Tales*, 'Here's God's plenty'. There are plenty of characters.

The novel begins with the description of Alu - who remains present in all the three sections of the novel. Alu, an eight-year-old boy, had lost his mother and father in a car accident and he comes to stay with an aunt Torudebi and uncle Balaram in Lalpukar. He does not know them at all. His is an extra-ordinary head,

> "huge several times too large for an eight year old boy". [3]

People tell about his head differently, but Bolaida says,

> "No, it is not like rock at all. It's an Alu, a potato; a huge fleshly lumpy potato". [3]

From that day, he is named Alu throughout the life though he had another name finely scriptural - Nachiketa Bose. He is neither ugly nor handsome, neither tall nor short, not even dark or fair. Instead of giving him a formal school education, Balaram decided to teach him the art of weaving. As he grows, he becomes perfect in this art. Being a victim of an integral trouble, Alu has to migrate from Calcutta to al-Ghazira. There too he becomes the only victim of the collapse of the star. After hard efforts fortunately he survives and leaves al-Ghazira with a new hope.

The other significant character in the novel is Balaram, a man of reason who applies logic to every small thing. The trouble with him is that theories come first and truth afterwards. He is interested in the school of Reason and establishes a school of practical reason and pure reason. He believes that every act of life has a purpose, so he establishes a third branch called March of reason. The novelist describes him as –

> "He has an ascetic face, with clean lines, a sharp ridge of a nose and wide, dreamy eyes. His high broad forehead rose to a majestic dome crowned with a thick, unruly pile of silver hair. It was an astonishing forehead: it glowed; it was like a lampshade for his bulging Higher Faculties-Language, Form, Number, the lot. It was a striking face even in repose: sometimes when he was animated, it was lit with such a bright pointed intensity that imprinted itself on the mind of everyone who saw him in those moments". [11]

To Bhudeo Roy Balaram is an extremist; an extremist who has no respect for order.

The novelist very minutely portrays Balaram's friend, Dantu, a rationalist. The name "Dantu" has history. As the novelist describes it:

> "His sharply domed head, of course, and his thin hollow face and those two long peeping front teeth from which he took his name. Besides, he always had the look of a saint." [14]

But Dantu's saintly look is deceptive. In the guide of a saint, he is a politician.

Balaram's neighbour and later on his enemy is Bhudeo Roy, Gopal, and Balaram's friend: a lawyer describes him thus:

> "He had looked like a fairly ordinary young man then, with thinning hair and a large pleasant face. He was a stout even then but far from fat, and in his starched white dhoti and kurta he had even possessed a certain kind of grace". [21]

Jyoti Das, an Assistant Superintendent of police, is an impressive character in the novel. He looks younger than his twenty-five years and that is a matter of pride for him. The novelist talks about him as follows –

> "a slight man of medium height, dark with straight black hair. He has a long even face with a rounded chin and a short, straight nose. His only irregular features are his eyebrows, which are slightly out of alignment. He is clean-shaven and prides himself on it, for it distinguishes him from his colleagues, who tend generally to be aggressively mustached. He is pleasant if not good-looking, and he looks younger than his twenty-five years. He is often mistaken for a college student". [123]

Shombhu Debnath a skillful weaver and Alu's teacher is a strong man with self respect:

> "He was tall, spectrally dark and skeletally thin. He was usually nearly naked, with only a thin *gamcha* wound around his waist, displaying proudly the corded muscles he bore all over him as a legacy of his years of weaving and wandering". [69]

Shombhu Debnath's son and Maya's brother, Rakhal is a man of dream and ambitions:

> "He was only sixteen, but already among the tallest in the village, and known everywhere for his skill with the bamboo pole. He had a special one for serious fights, studded with nails." [32]

The character of Rakesh appears in the second part of the novel. He, along with Alu, migrates from India to al-Ghazira for better prospects. Before that –

> "Rakesh was a traveling salesman for a small Ayurvedic pharmacy in Bhopal which specialized for a patented herbal laxative. It was the only job he had been able to find-despite his bachelor's Degree in commerce and that, too, only after a year's efforts". [182]

The most significant and attention-grabbing character in the novel is Jeevanbhai Patel – a businessman from Gujarat. The Durban Tailoring House belongs to him. Being a practical man, he constantly worships money. Money is both knowledge and power, he believes. Since he marries a Bohra girl, he is ostracized from his family. He moves from place to place, loses his name and fame, struggles a lot in his life, and after his wife's death once again he succeeds in establishing his business. He is the founder of New Life Marriage Bureau. He lives under the shadow of death and one day, he hangs himself with his belt, lonely without relatives.

The character of Nury, the egg seller, appears in the second section of the novel. He is a typical philosopher by nature. As the novelist says about him –

> "He had imagination. But more important, Nury was the only man in al-Ghazira who went from house to house everyday, talking to people, even to courtyards, taking in, in one glance as much as other people take in ten. Not a leaf fell, not a sheep shat in al-Ghazira without Nury's knowing of it. But all this he did quietly, for silence was in his nature". [248]

Prof. Samuel, an ex-accountant of a reputed firm is Rakesh's companion. He keeps account at Zindi's house–

> "He is not really a professor, of course. He was a teacher in some small town college, and as you know, at home every teacher whether he teaches pundits or pehlwans, is called a professor". [228]

The character of Dr. Mishra appears in the third section of the novel. Apart from being a doctor, he knows Sanskrit and Indian scriptures. He is a rationalist like Balaram. We perceive his genius when he says –

> "The world has come full circle: Carbolic acid has become holy water". [411]

The range of female characters varies from ordinary women like Nonderma to an educated professional woman like Dr. Uma Verma. Like the male characters, they too are struggling with life.

Nonderma, the maid servant of Balaram and Toru Debi, is an old widow who looks after Alu and does the household work at Balaram's home. As the novelist describes her -

> "Nonderma hobbled out of kitchen - mumbling toothlessly, bent almost double, no more than a few withered bones, with her widow's white homespun wrapped so carelessly around her that her dugs flapped outside, hanging down to her shrunken waist." [5]

Maya - the daughter of Shombhu Debnath and sister of Rakhal is an innocent character -

> "She was eleven then, a few months younger than Alu, but a good head taller and sturdily built. She had a red sari wound around her, covering her budding breasts. It was an old shrunken piece of cloth and it fell well short of her ankles and left her shoulder bare. She had a six-foot length bamboo in her hands. Her firm rounder face and her gently slanting eyes were dark with anger". [31-32]

Kulfi didi, a widow, is a tragic character of the novel. She is -

> "a fragile woman with long slender arms and a thin, hollowed - out face. Her cheeks looked as though they had collapsed, like a skin of a punctured drum". [175]

She does work as a cook in a rich family. She loses the job for trivial reasons. She dies of a heart attack and is buried like a Hindu woman in the sand of Sahara.

Zindi's character is fully developed by the novelist. She first came as a young and buxom beuty.hajj Fahmy an elderly man in Ras cared for her. She treats all strangers warmly. She is an interesting talker like every character in the novel. As the novelist affirms -

> "That was Zindi's power. She could bring together empty air and give it a body just by talking of it. They could never tire of listening to her speak, in her welter of languages, though they know every word, just as well as they know the lines of songs". [213]

Zindi is related with all the members who stay in her house. As she is growing older, she is worried about the maintenance of the house. She opines –

> "While everything is all right outside, things seem fine in the house-money keeps coming in and I can manage. But let something happen outside, and that is the end, there is nothing I can do? Why? Because I can give them food, I can give them a roof, but I can't give them work". [219]

Worried about the future of the migrants, she plans to buy the Durban Tailoring House. It does not materialize because of the death of Jeevanbhai Patel.

A friend to Zindi, Karthamma - an Indian woman who helps Zindi in household work:

> "She is tall woman, very dark, with the temper of an animal, but also an animal's courage for she was one person in the house who was never afraid to defy Zindi". [378]

the only educated and rational woman who appears in the third part of the novel, is Dr. Uma Verma. She is unorthodox and an emblem of the changing woman. She is a microbiologist, a sympathetic and warm hearted lady. She worries about humanity. She says –

> "All you ever talk about is rules. That's how you and your kind have destroyed everything - Science, Religion, Socialism with your rules and your orthodoxies. That's the difference between us: you worry about rules and I worry about being human". [409]

All the male and female characters of the novel are a product of the creator's mind. The discussion between Dr. Mishra and Uma beautifully focuses on Ghosh's art of characterization:

> "And when you do find something in a specimen can you really help wondering sometimes where all those microbes and bacteria and viruses come from? Whether they can really, all of them, be wholly external to our minds, they are anything than bodily metaphor for human pain and happiness or perhaps joy as well". [412]

What is remarkable for the readers is the opening of the novel. It stars with the arrival of the eight-year boy, Nachiketa in Balaram and Tori-debi's life, in Lalpukur village. The orphaned child of Balaram's brother is immediately nicknamed Alu since his head -

> "...... was an extraordinary head-huge, several times too large for an eight-eight year old, and curiously uneven, bulging all over with knots and bumps .... It is not like a rock at all. It's an Alu, a potato, a huge freshly dug, lumpy potato". [3]

The novel ends with Alu along with Zindi and Boss walking the streets of Medina upwards to the high battlements of the Kasbah waiting for Virat Singh's ship that would carry them home, to India. Though Alu enters the family of Balaram and Toru-debi, he remains on the periphery of the circle of this family. At Al-Ghazira, although he becomes part of Zindi's circle of friends and lodgers he remains detached from the group. In fact, he is an outsider both to Balaram who does not understand him and to Zindi who simply wants to help him since he appears confused and helpless.

The two circles of Balaram and Zindi are interconnected, on the one hand by the presence of Alu and on the other by sewing machine, carbolic acid and Alu's weaving skill. Balaram is passionately influenced by the book *Life of Pasteur* and develops a sense of cleanliness with the use of carbolic acid whereas Toru-debi is amorous of the sewing machine and her skill of tailoring blouses. Alu is taken up with weaving and learning new patterns from Shombhu Debnath. Amitav Ghosh weaves intricately the different and varied stories linking them through Alu and his childhood passions.

Though Ghosh calls Balaram a rationalist and a believer in science and reason, Balaram acts in a very irrational way. His favourite hobby is studying heads, phrenology which is no longer considered a science. His interest in the *Life of Pasteur* and the Rationalists' society is what Ghosh terms 'a Pasteurized Cosmos' –

> "It wasn't talk of reason, it wasn't the universal atom. It was passion: a passion which sprang from the simple and the every day. A passion for the future, not the past. It was that which made him [Pasteur] the greatest man of his time, for it is that passion which makes man great". [50]

It is the passion that makes Balaram attempt to clean the surrounding area in his village Lalpukur that brings about his doom, destruction and death. He starts a school called the school of reason but fails in his attempt to educate the village youths to think rationally. They are interested more in learning tailoring and weaving, the practical training of learning the skills for survival. He also fails in educating Alu since he refuses to attend the village school, though he loves to read books from Balaram's library. Balaram' s knowledge of Science and his faith in Reason have no base in real life situations. His is the abstract knowledge and knowledge without worldly wisdom is likely to bring about disaster. Balaram's behaviour at the time of Saraswati Puja, his passionate handling of the cleanliness movement with carbolic acid, and his love for the study of heads are ironically described. Ghosh seems to juxtapose the east against the west – with the practical learning of weaving and tailoring against the abstract ideology of rationalism. Toru-debi's practical sense and belief in the sewing machine saves Alu's life twice from the disaster created by Balaram's ideologies. When the machine stops working Toru-debi thrusts it into Alu's hands and asks him throw it away into the pond and get a new one for her -

> "Nothing's of any use now, she muttered. It's the end ..... She ran her hand over the machine's shining wheel and pulled, with all her strength. The wheel was absolutely rigid. She smiled at them: You see, he's haunted. There is something in him .... She lifted the black, sinuously carved machine off its wooden base and settled it on her lap, clucking to herself.... She stood up and put the machine in his [Alu's] arms. Throw it into the pond, she said. It's dead ..... get me another, Alu, my bit of gold, won't you?" [147-148]

When Alu runs into the forest with the machine, he suddenly finds that fire has broken out at Balaram's house, his home and wants to go back, but is prevented by Bolai-da who thereby saves his life. The fire was caused by Balaram's plan of attack on Bhudeo Roy with the help of Rakhal. He was prepared:

> "Balaram had spent the right in the canvas shelter he had rigged upon the dust path which ran past his house to Bhudeb Roy's. It was surrounded by a circle of heavy oil-drums with an opening where the circle met the path, which ran to the front door of his house. The shelter was only a canvas sheet stretched over the drums, and held in place by stones ..... [136] and once again he rehearsed his plan: all he had to do was reach Bhudeo Roy with one burst of Carbolic, only one, and he would turn and run as fast as his legs would carry him. That was all. His stomach churned: but would it work?" [138]

Nothing mattered to him. He is so passionately involved that for him,

> "nothing existed now but the ecstasy of waiting for the climax, the discovery at hand. Did Pasteur have an inkling of this terrifying joy when he went to examine Joseph Meister the morning after he had inoculated him with his untested vaccine?"

Ghosh has painted this picture of Balaram's ecstasy, showing how ironical the situation is. Instead of the discovery and Bhudeb Roy's humiliation, what Balaram finds is the engulfing fire that breaks out. It is through Alu's eyes that we glimpse this:

> "...... brilliant Sunburst of light arced into the sky and the whole forest shimmered in the eerie silver glow. He [Alu] saw it reach its zenith and curve downwards and fall out of his sight, behind the bamboo ...... And then the earth shook and the air seemed to come alive and hit him with walls of force, and when he opened his eyes again and exactly where the house ought to have been there were orange flames shooting into the sky". [148]

Balaram and everything and everybody around him is engulfed by the fire. It is this rationalist and scientific mind of Balaram that brings about his destruction and death. Pasteur has discovered a life-saving drug but Balaram's knowledge brings death. In fact, Ghosh presents the folly of obsession by his limited knowledge of scientific inventions of the Western Science.

The same Carbolic and creates trouble in al-Ghazira when the 'displaced' persons living with around Zindi decide to clean every house and shop. Zindi is the only person who does not believe in this cleanliness movement. Whey they take out a sort of procession and try to clean shops and stores in this foreign place, the police shoot them and most of them of die. Only Alu, Zindi, Kulfi and the child Boss are saved. Here, it is Alu who talks about Carbolic acid, cleanliness and money. Saved from the rubble of the collapsed building star, Alu lectures them about money. Buried under the two sewing machines, he is happily thinking about life and death. Unlike Nachiketa of the Mahabharat who had returned from Yama the Lord of death after acquiring knowledge about life and death, Alu thinks of only purity and dirt. Nachiketa had gained the philosophy of life. This Nachiketa i.e. Alu returns from death's door, but his knowledge only brings destruction. He talks about Louis Pasteur and his failure [280] as Balaram had done earlier. But Alu believes that he has acquired real / true knowledge:

> "There, in the ruins, he [Alu] had discovered what it was that Pasteur had really wanted all his life - an intangible thing, something he had not understood himself, yet a thing the whole world had conspired to deny him.

Purity, Purity was what he had wanted, purity and cleanliness - not just his home, or in a laboratory or a university, but in the whole world of living men. It was that which spurred him on his greatest hunt, the chase in which he drove the enemy of purity, the quintessence of dirt, the demon which keeps the world from cleanliness ..... the Infinitely Small, the Germ". [280]

And tells the spellbound crowd that this Germ is Money. 'No money, no dirt' [280]. These people who are illegally in al-Ghazira to earn money and send it back home to their family, are carried away by the eloquence of Alu [since he has returned from death's door] and are ready to form a sort of 'Co-operative' and thereby save something more than they individually could do. It is Zindi who is down to earth and has practical knowledge of the value of money in a foreign country and who refuses to join this mad movement of the mob. Ghosh once again appears to ridicule the mob of psychology of the people mesmerized by Alu's speech. The common Indian belief that money is the root cause of all evil / sin is paradoxically presented. On the one hand, these people have arrived at the oil-city of al-Ghazira illegally to try their hand at earning more money.

On the other hand, they are prepared to hand over their earning to the Professor for safe-keeping. Alu is depicted here as a saint who preaches and teaches about the evils of money. Alu who was once a silent person, a passive character and who acted according to what others told him to, is so very eloquent that people believe every word he utters. Alu who is a silent observer and keeps weaving continuously, is shown in contrary colours. Only his discovery of 'dirt and purity' makes him lecture to the willing crowd who are impressed as he is the 'chosen one' of the Gods. Alu survives the chaos, destruction and death once again and finds himself following Zindi, Kulfi and the child Boss. Zindi had already arranged a passage for leaving al-Ghazira where they were no longer safe. And all this was Alu's doing.

Going from one place to other, continent to continent, Ghosh's characters are kept floating in the novel. They even do not form any relationship worth the name. They keep telling their stories, trying to link up plot of the novel, but to little avail. Ghosh does not probe deep into their minds. The ghetto at al-ghazira is very picturesquely described. Every character is given a tale but no habitation, nor roots. They remain fable-characters, passively listening to each other's stories and not acting positively in a significantly way. The post-modernist tendency is to show what they are and not who they are. As K. Damodar Rao in '*Magic and Irony as Principles of Structure* - A Reading of *The Circle of Reason*' puts it -

> "In *The Circle of Reason*, the attempts of the novelist are obviously oriented to floating the events and characters through a medley of metaphors and select ideas". [32]

Every character tells the story of his experience, but the style of narrating the story is never distinct. It is quite obvious that the novelist himself in fact, tells characters' tales. Ghosh tries to weave together the different stories through references to sewing machines, Carbolic acid, *Life of Pasteur,* money and dirt, purity and cleanliness, rationalism and science. He utilizes all these devices to make a coherent whole of the novel. It is Alu that he keeps as a living link. And yet Alu is never the centre of Balaram's story, nor of Zindi's and certainly not of Dr. Uma Verma's. If Balaram's obsession with science, rationalism, Carbolic acid and *Life of Pasteur* makes him a character out of comic fantasy, Zindi's practically Alu's love for weaving is the only metaphor that binds and weaves the episodes together. The knowledge that Balaram and Alu acquire is not the life-giving, life-sustaining knowledge, but an abstract knowledge that is far removed from the realities of life. Balaram's is the knowledge of the western science and ideology and Alu's is the eastern philosophy of considering money as dirt. Both are mocked at. Inspite of the destruction and death they bring about, the impression that is created is not one of serious tragedy but of comic misfortune. Only Alu's practical knowledge of Weaving, related to life-sustaining forces brings hope. In *The Calcutta Chromosome* too, Ghosh pitches knowledge / science of the West against the intuition / counter science of the east.

The novel *The Circle of Reason* begins with Alu who was orphaned with the death of his parents in the car accident. Alu moves on from disaster to disaster. He moves on from the shattering death of his uncle and aunt in a fire, onwards to the death and destruction of his fellow-friends at al-Ghazira and finally to Kulfi's death from heart-attack. Alu witnesses nothing, but death and disaster. Ghosh hints at the hope, yes, hope for the bird-watcher police officer, Jyoti Das, hope for Zindi with the child Boss and her profession. But what for Alu? He returns home but what home has he in India? His skill as a weaver, a creative activity may help him survive. The novel remains a question mark. In Alu's life there are no choices. He drifts from place to place and person to person without any will, desire or effort on his part. But it is not a rounding off. As Fry had maintained that the fiction is but an entrée to a gracious *Mansfield Park* or a cluttered *Bleak House* or one may add a chaotic passionate world of *The Circle of Reason.* To talk in the words of Irving H. Buchen –

> "It is not a little to say that the novel is more a way of traveling than a point of arrival; more an invitation to wander than a secure niche, and more akin to the way a man enters and meanders through this world than to an assured resting place in the after life". [32]

What is expected is a journey from purpose to passion perception. There is too much passion but too little of perception. What one finds in *The Circle of Reason* is a sort of uncertainty of perception or meaning.

WORKS CITED

Ghosh, Amitav. *The Circle of Reason,* London : Hamish Hamilton Ltd., 1986.

Rao, Damodar K. 'Magic and Irony as Principles of Structure : A Reading of *The Circle of Reason'*, in R. K. Dhawan's *The Novels of Amitav Ghosh,* New Delhi: Prestige Books, 1999.

Buchen, Irvin H. '*The Aesthetics of the Supra-novel* in John Halperin's [ed] *The Theory of Novel,* New York: Oxford University Press, 1974.

Bhatt, Indira and Indira Nityanandam. *The Fiction of Amitav Ghosh,* New Delhi: Creative Books, 2001.

www.time.com/time/2005/100books/the _complete-list.html.

www.geogianencyclopedia.org.http://www.georgianencyclopedia.org/nge/Article.jsp?id=h-2895.

www.schweitzwe.org.http://www.schweitzwe.org/english/aseind.html.

www.iblict.com/http://iblict.com/author611.html.

3

The Shadow Lines

Amitav Ghosh in *The Shadow Lines* has beautifully woven the fact and fiction in a complex, absorbing the story that shows lives across nations and spans almost half a century of recent Indian history. The reader looks at love and loyalty and examines the questions of fidelity and accountability, of tradition and modernity, of freedom and its evanescent quality.

As the British Empire finished, and division through lines of Indian subcontinent, thousands were exiled. The changes brought about in three generations of a Bengali family spread up across three countries as a result of historical changes in the land is the focus of this novel: it brings out the confusion and the trauma of the East Bengal *shikkhita madhyabitta* [the educated middle class] uprooted and lost after the dismembering of Bengal in 1947.

The novel is divided into two parts, *'Going Away'* and *'Coming Home.'* The novel beautifully shifts from past to present and from present to past, Ghosh manages in a masterly way time of two kinds, time past: memory and time present: reality. The first section *'Going Away'* means *'going away from self, 'Coming Home'* means *'Coming back in the self'*. The concept of coming and going not belonging more often than the belonging is expressed as part of the family's secret lore because –

> "You see, in our family we don't know whether we're coming or going - it's all my grandmother's fault. But of course, the fault wasn't hers at all : it lay in language. Every language assumes a centrality, a fixed and settle point to go away from and come back to and what my grandmother was looking for was a word for a journey which was not a coming or a going at all a journey that was a search for precisely that fixed point which permits the proper use of verbs of movement." [153]

So, one is constantly plagued by doubts in the novel as to whether the characters are going to Calcutta or coming to Calcutta or coming to London or going back to London. The two sections of the Novel clearly indicate this enigma of having to decide where home is Calcutta or Dhaka [Bangladesh] or London. When home is an uncertain place, borders too compound the problem.

The first section *'Going Away'* ends with the narrator's coming face-to-face Ila's indifference towards him. It also ends on a note that Ha possessed his life and her going, away meant death to him. The second section *'Coming Home'* ends with the narrator's regaining self-possession, his getting over his love for Ila, union with May and acceptance of Tridib's death.

The novel is full of symbolic references to Houses old and new, maps and mirrors, borders and boundaries. All these symbols in one way or the other deal with the theme of man's search for identity, his search for roots. This is not a story of the grandmother but it is a story of the eternal suffering of every man torn between the past and the present. The novel raises serious question about roots, identities, war, borders and so on –

> "I would have been frightened she said. But I would have prayed for strength, and Good Willing, yes, I

> would have killed him. It was for or freedom. I would have done anything to be free." [39]

These are the words exclaimed by the nameless grandmother. Amitav Ghosh in *The Shadow Lines* about partition and immigration explores man's eternal quest for freedom. He clearly shows that it is not humanly possible to be totally free. One can only attempt it. Though all the characters in the novel exhibit an urge to be 'free' none of them is totally free in the end. 'Freedom' therefore means a number of competing discourses that cannot be mistaken for a single metaphysical state. The narrator voices the impossibility of attaining complete freedom -

> "If freedom were possible, surely Tridib's death would have set me free. And yet; all it takes to set my hand shaking like a leaf, fifteen years later, thousands of miles away at the other end of another continent, is a chance remark by a waiter in a restaurant." [239]

The novel is a powerful adolescent love story and a story of unrequited love. The narrator realizes that Ila would never love him as he loved her. Tridib also loved May but May was never sure of her love for him. Nick Price is May's brother whom Ila loved. Ila always pretended that Nick was her knight in shining armour, but Nick betrayed her as a child and subsequently as an adult Ila tries hard to discard her Indianness. She wanted to go to nightclub in Calcutta where she wanted to drink and dance. Her cousin Robi did not allow her and hurt, she says -

> "Do you see now I've chosen to live in London? Do you see? It's only because I want to be free. Free of your bloody culture and free of all you." [88-89]

It is surprising that Ila with her upper middle class values marries a person who does not love her and who is a wastrel. It is strange that she just want to skim the surface of life.

The novel tells the story of three generations of the narrator's family spread over Calcutta, Dhaka [Bangladesh] and London and lines up characters from different nationalities, religion and cultures in the world. The grandmother, Jethamoshai, Mayadebi and Shaheb are representatives of the first generation, the Father, the Mothers, Jatin are eccentric representatives of the second generation, Ila, Nick, May and the Narrator are representative of the third generation.

The third situation is portrayed when May and the Narrator lie together in London in 1979, on the eve of the Narrator's return to India. All the three situations are presented specifically after violent happenings in Dhaka. Ghosh portrays violence affected far off places both in Time and Space only to give meaning to love making, the reality of life, force and to show how Tridib, May and the Narrator grow mature in Understanding and attain redemption through Love. The situations are the same but the players are different. Both May and the Narrator find release from the mystery of Tridib's death a sacrificial offering as May calls it, which cannot be explained or understood.

> "Do you 1hink I killed him? she said. I stayed silent. I did not want to answer her. I used to think so too, she said I though I'd killed him".
>
> "I was safe you see. I could have gone right into that mob, and they wouldn't have touched me, an English membership but he, he must have known he was going to die.... He gave himself up. It was a sacrifice. I know I can't understand it, I know I mustn't try, for any real sacrifice is a mystery." [151-152]

In short, Amitav Ghosh's work seems to move effortlessly across national frontiers, as Robert Dixon puts it not inhabiting -

> "a culture rooted in a single place, but a discursive space that flows across political and national

> boundaries and even across generations in time." [Dixon, Rovert: 1996: 9]

Ghosh believes in the issue of identity that lies at the heart of democracy. Perhaps this issue of identity could be traced to the story of 1947, which according to Ritu Menon and Kamla Bhasin is –

> "a gendered narrative of displacement and dispossession, of large-scale and widespread communal violence, and of the realignment of family, community and national identities as people were forced to accommodate the dramatically altered reality that now prevailed". [1993: ws2]

Ghosh finds the concept and meaning of the protagonist's freedom and identity – the theme very close to the modern man. Political freedom was the most memorable event that happened in 1947 when India got her freedom. Equality and freedom were granted to all the citizens of this country, irrespective of caste, creed or sex. By liberating themselves of the shackles of the British Empire, people thought, that they had achieved something prestigious, that the Empire had denied them – the freedom of the individual.

The Shadow Lines is a masterpiece in the contemporary Indo-English Literature. It leaves a lasting impression on the reader, with its structural intricacies and brilliance and thematic profundity. The main events of the novel take place in England, India and Pakistan during the turbulent times of war, communal riots and resulting ethos of uncertainty and inexplicable fear. Throughout the novel, the reader experiences a nagging threat of the forces of friction and destruction. The artificiality crated and politically maneuvered barriers between nation and nation, people and people, need to be transcended beyond the confines of time and space. Tridib's life and death bring out the tragic irony of the inescapable duality of the human mind. His spirit of Liberation is both triumph and a defeat, of his creative imagination and selfless love.

The novel no doubt tries to bring out the inner paradox of Tridib's life, and his efforts to overcome that. Tridib is a student of archaeology with deep interest in history. He can perceive not only 'the pastness of the past', but also live the pastness in the present. His 'imaginative eye' can see the permanent in the transient and explode all the artificial barriers of time and space. It escapes the bondage that limits ordinary human consciousness. He is the narrator's uncle by family relations. But a more profound emotional bond binds them. He is the narrator's 'idealized hero' and 'a mentor'. Tridib's search for the ideal world is kept alive by his nephew even after the former's death. Tridib's passionate dream of a completely integrated inner and outer world is expressed thus:

> "..... One could never knew anything except through desire, real desire ..... a pure, painful and primitive desire, a longing for everything that was not in one's self a torment of the flesh, that carried one beyond the limits of one's mind to another place and even, if one was lucky, to a place where there was no order between oneself and one's image in the mirror". [29]

This intense longing for 'everything that was not in oneself' and 'a place without any border' is almost like a hermit's speech for 'Adwait'. But paradoxically this passion for the ideal world is counter balanced in his real life by a detached and restrained attitude. He is introduced to the reader as 'a recluse' 'happiest in the neutral territory' of the strangers, 'most himself outside home' etc. Like Camus's 'Outsider', he is estranged and lonely. He does not submit to the narrow confines of time, place or person. He retains his freedom through creative inventions and the power of active imagination. He tells the narrator:

".... We could not see without inventing what we saw, so at least we could try to do it properly ... we had to try because the alternative wasn't blankness.... It only meant that if we didn't try ourselves, we would never be free of other people's inventions". [31]

There can be no inventions without imagination. But it is absolutely necessary to use it with 'precision', with great care and responsibility. The danger of succumbing to other people's invention is as threatening as the danger of 'improper imaginings', 'irresponsible inventing'. In order to gain and retain the real freedom, the mind has to first realize the true meaning of responsibility.

Tridib's words are a warning to all those who evade such a responsibility of owning a life of individual commitment. Groups do not have any consciousness. They only obey rules and they are determined. An individual soul can transcend this bondage through individual consciousness. Today, when we live under the constant threat of being invaded by the exploitative strategies of the power structures, unless an individual makes an honest and desperate effort to escape them, he is likely to fall their Victim. The freedom from 'other people's inventions' requires, almost demands, a moral compulsion to keep the search for the knowledge of the Real, eternally alive. And yet, it is a tragic irony of the finite human life, that the Absolute always escapes its grasp.

"The seductive ...... clarity is an illusion of knowledge. Tridib is fully aware of this tragic irony and is not free from despair because he cannot imagine what it would be like to confront the most real of [their] realities" [67].

It is this reality of the knowledge of Death, which is most difficult to confront. He says -

> "The realities of the bombs and torpedoes and the dying was easy enough to imagine-mere events, after all, recording in thousands of films and photographs and comic books. But not that infinitely more important reality: the fact that they themselves would not survive the war. What is the colour of that knowledge? Nobody knows, nobody can ever know, not even in memory, because there are moments in time that are not knowable ....". [67-68]

It is this knowledge of the 'unknowable moments in

time; the unfathomable mystery of the human mind, that keeps Tridib humble and lonely. The tragic awareness is reflected in his most painful cry: "What is the colour of that knowledge?" Tridib knows that the colour will always be unclear and hazy, human knowledge will always be tentative, elusive, and arbitrary. This awareness makes him 'an eternal stranger' like Camus' Outsider, whose detached attitude to the world conceals a more tragic paradox of 'the duality' - the simultaneous awareness of both - a need to find meaning of life and the futility of such a search. Nevertheless, against all the nihilistic forces, Tridib continues his eternal search.

Like his earlier desire 'to be free from other people's inventions, Tridib expresses a more subtle need to experience freedom in love. He desires the complete freedom of 'A stranger', for he knows that this estrangement keeps the mind free from any presuppositions. In his letter to May Price, an English friend from a very young age and lover in maturity, he expresses his wish:

> ".... to meet her, May as a stranger in ruin ..... to meet as the completest of strangers - stranger-across-the-sea all the more strangers because they knew each other already". [144]

This paradox of being 'more strangers because they knew each other already' is the same ironical awareness that the clarity in knowledge is only an illusion - in reality each remains an island, as strangers, not only the other, but even to one's own self. But, Tridib does not allow this awareness to dissuade him from the world of imagination and inventions. He can 'live in the story' when he chooses to.

Tridib's favourite story of Tristan is a sad tale of a lover waiting for his love 'across-the-sea'. A story is an escape into an imaginary world. Tridib first heard it, 'to hold back his tears', and to combat a much terrifying fear of the war. Then, it was passed on to the younger generation – the story is a universal metaphor for man's eternal search for the ideal and his inability to attain it in real life. However, this paradox is transcended through imaginative inventions. According to him, people live in stories.

Tridib finds his fulfillment in love as a stranger-in-the-ruin, during May's visit to Calcutta. The narrator, May and Tridib went to see the Memorial. May could not bear the sight of it and blurted out:

> "It shouldn't be here...... it's an act of violence. It is obscene .... No, it's not, he [Tridib] said, This is our ruin; That's what we've been looking for". [170]

They held each other's hands with tender loving care in perfect communication. This is the strength of true love. It can transcend the violations and oppressions of human history. The monument is a remainder of the colonial Rule / Oppression f the past. However, it does not dissuade these two 'strangers-across-the-sea' from loving each other. Their love is suggestive of the possible triumph of the present union over the past evil. If man can forget and forgive the past evils and transcend the artificial barriers, allow his mind to be free from the presuppositions of the past, he may be able to achieve an ideal world. Finally, it is nature and circumstances of Tridib's death that suggests a possible meaning to this seemingly meaningless life. Against all the nihilistic forces, he stands up as a positive force of hope and faith in the strength of true love.

During the communal riots in 1964 in India and Pakistan, Tridib visited Dhaka with May and his aunt. While trying to save the lives of his granduncle and a poor rickshaw -driver, he lost his life at the hands of a few fanatics. When the frenzied mob attacked the old man and rickshaw-driver, May, Tridib and the others saw this from a moving car. May first jumped out of the car and rushed towards the victims. Tridib instantly followed her and soon overtook her. He plunged into the crowd and 'vanished'. Later, May found three dead bodies, Tridib's being one. For years, May carried the guilt of Tridib's killing, till a deeper and more humble realization dawned upon her. She said:

> "For years, I was arrogant enough to think I owned him his life. But, I know now I didn't kill him: I couldn't have, if I'd wanted to. He gave himself up : it was a sacrifice. I can't understand it, I know I mustn't try, for any real sacrifice is a mystery." [251-252]

May's disowning the responsibility of Tridib's death is a tribute to the latter's dignified self-sacrifice. The ultimate mystery of such a sacrifice will often elude definition - for who can fathom the depth of a martyr's mind? May's confession only suggests that Tridib did not die for any petty, selfish desire, but rather he gave himself up for his belief and conviction. However, the irony behind his tragic death cannot be negated. When anarchic forces, and the ordinary reality surround the world is only arbitrary and contingent, can one say with certainty that his sacrifice was meaningful? However, one pays the highest tribute to his courage of conviction.

On the whole, the character of Tridib projects a true spirit of individual freedom. It is human privilege and responsibility to keep his spirit of liberation eternally alive. In this increasingly hostile world of wars, violence, frictions, divisions, where -

> "there are only states and citizens; there are no people at all". [223]

Tridib's life and death suggest a possible subversion of such hostile forces. Hatred alienates and dehumanizes people. It is time to give up violence and curb the further deterioration. Tridib echoes Philip Larkin's faith:

> "What will survive of us is Love".

Besides this, the novel no doubt portrays a powerful

adolescent love story and a story of unrequited love. The narrator realizes that Ila would never love him as he loved her. Tridib also loved May, but May was never sure of her love for him. Ila was the narrator's cousin, a diplomat's daughter who had travelled all over the world. Ila lived a fancy life, she wore modern clothes, her language was different and to the narrator, she was 'like no girl I'd never seen before except in pictures in American Magazines'. But Ila is untouched by all the places she has travelled to, unlike the narrator who is totally fascinated. For Ila, Cairo was a place where 'Ladies' was on the other side of the departure lounge. It was another fault that she could not understand, for as Tridib often said of her -

> "the inventions she lived in moved with her, so that although she lived in many places, she had never travelled at all" [76].

All that she would get while her family came back, for their annual holidays was the year book of the international school, she was currently attending and she would invent stories of her being the heroine of the school. Most of her stories would be about Nick Price, May's brother whom Ila loved. Ila often pretended that Nick was her knight in shining armour, but Nick betrayed her as a child and subsequently as an adult. That is when, the narrator realizes that he could never mean as much to Ila as she meant to him:

> "Naked in force of that unthinkable adult truth, that need is not transitive that one may need without being needed." [78]

Ila tries hard to discard her Indianness. She wanted to go to a nightclub in Calcutta where she wanted to drink and dance. Her cousin, Robi did not allow her and hurt, she screams,

> "I want to be free of you, free of your bloody culture and that is why I live in London". [89]

It is a contrast to the narrator who begins to wonder whether he was mad because he was happy in being bound:

> "Whether I was alone in knowing that I could not live without the clamour of the voices within me" [90].

Even, the grandmother feels that Ila does not know the meaning of freedom because she wants to be left alone to do exactly what she pleases.

But inspite of all these differences, the narrator loves her and Ila thinks of him as the brother she never has. The narrator wonders:

> "love is utterly alien to that other idea without which we can not live as human beings, to the idea of justice, love is so profoundly the enemy of justice". [123]

Unfortunately for Ila who tries to discard her Indianness and lives in London, sharing her flat with a bearded Irish computer scientist, a girl from Leicester, 'morose young Ghanian who was very active in the anti-Nazi league', she is never accepted as one of them by her flat-mates. They regard her as a decorative piece and a kind of guest. And Ila in her shortsightedness and superficial thinking, thought that living abroad made her superior to the narrator. She appeared immeasurably distant then in her serene confidence, in the centrality and eloquence of her experience, in her quiet pity for the pettiness of lives like mine, lived out in the silence of voiceless events in a backward world. But the narrator knows –

> "but still I had known people of my own age, who had survived the great terror in the Calcutta of the sixties and seventies. I thought I had at least the spectator's knowledge of their courage, something that Ila with her fine clothes and manicured hands would Never understand". [112]

Though there was dichotomy, once Ila had come out

of the Hairdresser shop, her hair all new and curled and marched straight off to Brixton with her little group of friends to confront a gang of jack-booked racists armed with bicycle chains. And the narrator realized he could have never done that.

It is much later in the novel, that the narrator makes his love for Ila obvious. But Ila says her voice full of pity that 'you are like the brother I never had'. That's when the narrator writes,

> "I knew she had taken my life hostage again, I knew that a part of my lie as a human being had ceased that I no longer existed but as a chronicle". [132]

Ila and Nick get married and the narrator mourns it by getting drunk. Nick has already shown his true colours, he is living off her and yet is blatantly unfaithful to her. An unhappy Ila confides in the narrator and speaks of her love for Nick. She also tells the narrator that she is as chaste as any 'bhartiya nari', and the things she told the narrator in Calcutta were only for shock value. She also adds that she loves Nick so much that she would never leave him and will always put up with his infidelities. Of course, Ila never lets Nick forget that he is living off her and makes it a point to talk about it. The narrator visualizes Nick's future –

> "helpless, depedence coupled with despairing little acts of rebellion". "I remember what May had said about him, he is different, not like us". [133]

It is surprising that Ila with her upper middle class values marries a person who does not love her and who is a wastrel. She, with her best exposure to life, does not want to further her life or her career, and is happy living of her father. It is stranger that she just wants to skim the surface of life. Even when she starts working for a child-organization, she is emotionally so dishonest because she hates small children. It is difficult to understand why Amitav Ghosh has portrayed Ila as such a superficial person.

May is portrayed in a more humane and sensitive manner. Her relationship with Tridib's remains unconsummated due to Tridib's untimely brave and sacrificial death. Tridib sees May as a little baby when he went to England with his parents in 1939. They meet later in India in 1964, but their friendship through correspondence has ripened into love about which Tridib is certain, and May is still confused. Tridib's love for May is manifest in his letters to her. He wanted them to meet-

> "as the completest of strangers-strangers across the seas, all the more strangers because they knew each other already. He wanted them to meet far from their friends and relatives in a place without past, without history, free, really free, two people coming together the utter freedom of strangers". [144]

May is not very sure of her feelings. She is angry with Tridib's letter. Yet she wants to visit India though she convinces herself it has nothing to do with Tridib, but was just plain curiosity. But when she sees Tridib in person,

> "she knew at last why she had come and she was glad, it had nothing to do with curiosity". [135]

May and Tridib meet in Calcutta and their love for each other is described through the eyes of the child narrator:

> "Why do I remember the incident ..... because of the way they looked at each other perhaps, the way he touched her and she kissed the palm of his hand, the way they smiled as though there was a secret between them that I could never understand". [153]

But when the grown up narrator meets May in London, he asks her about her feelings for Tridib and May says,

> "I don't know, how can you expect me to know? What right have you got to ask me that? What right have you got to ask me that? What do you think I have been asking myself these last seventeen years?

> I don't know whether any of it is real, whether I was in love with him or merely fascinated by the sense of defeat that surrounded him. I was so young then". [143]

And as far as Tridib is concerned,

> "all I remember is him saying you are my love, my own true love my own. true love, my love across the seas; what do I have to do to keep you with me". [154]

It is May who tells the narrator the real cause of Tridib's death, how he sacrificed himself in Dhaka in those communal riots. At first, May had lived with the guilt that she was the cause of his death, but now she realizes, that she was not the cause,

> "but now I know, I didn't kill him, I couldn't have if I had wanted. He gave himself up, it was a sacrifice. I know I didn't understand it, I know I mustn't try, for any real sacrifice is a mystery". [166]

May's character is shown as very different from that of Ila. The child narrator remembers when May was very keen to hear the cotton man's instrument. When he mentioned this to Ila, she dismissed it by saying –

> "She has kind of wide-eyed air about her even when she is in London like one of those worthy women who come down from small towns on weekend return tickets". [166]

But the grown up narrator says looking back at the incident –

> "May's curiosity had grown out of a kind of innocence, an innocence which set her apart from all the women I know for it was not the innocence of ignorance, but a forthright unworldly kind of innocence which I had never met in a woman for among the women I knew like my mother and her relatives there were none,

> no matter how secluded, who were free of that peculiar worldliness which comes from dealing with large families, a trait which seemed to grow in those women in direct proportion to the degree to which they were secluded from the world". [167]

May minces no words in describing her own brother Nick as dishonest unlike Ila who is always trying to portray Nick as something he is not. May is working for an organization whose cause she believes in. She is still happy working at grassroots levels. She is brave enough to kill the dog who is in agony and Tridib does tell her "promise you'll do it for me, if ever need be". [167]

The younger May had all the impetuousness and heady idealism of youth. She believed in the rightness of her cause. Tridib's decision to follow her is in keeping with his not being a man of action. If he had yanked her back into the car, he would not have been Tridib. His imagination was fired by her boldness and he followed her in a daze not quite comprehending what might happen. But the older May is too good:

> "a kind of a caricature of a do-gooder than as a realistic portrait". [175]

But somehow, May still has some ambition and strength of character, while Ila is shown as a woman with no strength of character, while Ila is shown as a woman with no strength of character and no ambition. It is strange because the modern woman in most recent novels is portrayed as a survivor. No matter what culture, what upbringing, they are survivors and achievers. They all go through life realizing that at the end of the day only they themselves can help themselves. It is an 'introspective realization of self dependency' [168].

Besides the depiction of these significant characters, Amitav Ghosh presents the novel a s a perfect specimen of partition. It has the story woven around the narrator's grandmother, Tridib, Ila, May Price with the pendulum of memory swinging from past into present and back into the past. Each and every character's work and action leaves an imprint on the mind on the other characters thereby helping the novel to grow and surpass the rigid barrier of time, place and action. Memory works in the direction of family histories restructured in search of meaning.

The story of the novel compels the reader to feel and perceive various delicate issues like partition, interpersonal relationships, religious cults. The narrator was often in awe of his cousin Tridib and looked upon him as a role model. Ila his niece, who had been brought up in an aristocrat atmosphere of London, loved nothing but 'her freedom' which Indian culture always denied her. May Price - an alien possessed love for India - would be going to Delhi and Agra first and then to Calcutta before flying to Dhaka. But the most impressive character who helps the narrative to weave around the concept of memory and socio political situation is grandmother, who after serving as Headmistress has retired and begins her journey on the roads of the faded memories. Remembering her house in Dhaka, which was like a huge, step pyramid inhibited by so many branches of the family that even the most knowledgeable amongst them had become confused about their relationships.

The ghost of bygone times often continued to cling to every person in this novel, which never permits the novelist to lose touch with the fact that the memory forms the bases of the entire novel -

> "I cannot remember when it happened, any more than I remembered when I first learnt to tell the time or tie my shoe lace". [3]

At the very beginning of the novel, the view of the narrator and the novelist is very clear. The transfiguration of the memory not only helps the narrator to march forward, but also links the narration to the changing time and scenarios -

> "When I go past Gole Park now I often wonder that the world is close to me. Montu went away to America

> and Nathu Ram Chaubey went beck to Banaras to start a hotel. Now there is a crowd thronging through these neon lit streets, the air conditioned shops filled with rickety stalls. At that time in the early sixties there were so few cars around there that we thought nothing of paying football on the streets around the roundabout. Gole Park was considered somewhat to be outside Calcutta. In school, it was thought that I catch a train every morning as though I lived in a far-flung refuge camp on the border". [8]

A shadow line hovers between imagination and reality. The interpersonal relationships are partly based on imagination and partly on reality, and when they are retold they are re-lived as well. The narrator's silent love for Ila often made him have a protective disposition towards her. Ila according to grandmother's thinking is –

> "a greedy slut, who was living in America only for money and comforts". [79]

But the narrator's love often shielded her from all these accusations of the grandmother,

> "She has to live on pocket money; she doesn't have the memory to buy things. She spends her time going on demonstrations and acting plays to Indian immigrants in East London". [79]

If the childhood love made him feel bowled by the charm of Ila, the adolescent love made him more concerned for her,

> "She was crying very hard. I put an arm around her and held her tight against me. I knew she wanted to tell me something". [187]

In this novel, the meaning of what happened is the central issue. People and events encountered in childhood are brought into focus when the adult narrator views them from a perspective of cumulative knowledge. The child's involvement in the relationship of Ila with Nick and that of May and Tridib takes him to the threshold of awareness and the fresh perceptive heightens his sensitivity to the deeper meaning.

The love of May and Tridip could not be a success and ended in a tragedy, but it attained a 'samaritan' attribute, for Tridib had given up his life to save May from the riotous mob which had mad May comment years after on his death -

> "For years I was arrogant enough to think I owned him his life. But I know now I didn't kill him. It was a sacrifice. I know I mustn't try to understand, for any real sacrifice is a mystery". [252]

Tridib and May's love was paradoxical. If found it was on the bedrock of pornographic letters or cupping her chin in his palms it also revealed unselfish and devoted love when to save May from the furious crowd he had laid down his life. His death coincided with the death of that dog whose throat was slit by May followed by the promise taken from her by Tridib,

> "Promise me you'll do it for me too if I should ever need it". [174]

The narrator was grateful to May for the glimpse she had given him of the final redemptive mystery of Tridib's death and which had been haunting Robi,

> "Ever since it had happened and the memory of it would never go, it stayed. I used to think that if only it would go away, I would be free. I would have given anything to be free of that memory". [246]

As stated before, the relationships are caught inexorably in the web of complexities. Another relationship was that of Ila and Nick [first being May and Tridib]. The narrator's memory of their relationship strikes the reader as sometimes immature and sometimes based on comprise. What Ila tells, the narrator speaks the statement loudly-

> "He told me the woman who answered the phone was from Martinique. He met her in a pub and he's been seeing her for a year or two. He's got an Indonesian woman in line too and there's me, of course. But I can't leave him. I love him so much that I could never leave him". [189]

Remarkable is the memory of the same that Ila speaks about Nick towards the end of the novel -

> "You mustn't pay attention to what I said the other day. I was just overwrought. Nick wouldn't dream of doing anything that would upset me. You mustn't believe me. I made it all up. It's fine now. We're taking a little holiday". [248]

It is also noteworthy that the narrator maintains relationship with Tridib with full of nostalgia, awe and wonder -

> "I ran all the way to the park, but if I happened to hear that Tridib was around I would double back through the park and back lanes. I was grateful for the small privileges his presence secured for me on those streets for the odd sweet given to me by the shop-keeper of his acquaintance, from being rescued from the fight in the park by some young fellow who knew him. When he would begin to hold fourth on all kinds of subject - East European jazz, the play of Gracia Lorca, I would be close bursting with pride". [9]

The narrator remembers that he had not seriously taken the new of Tridib's death initially because of this relationship,

> "He [father] expected me to burst into tears but for me 'dead' was just the word associated with films and comic books. I had no means of attaching that word to a real presence like Tridib. I felt nothing. No shock, no grief." [239]

"The manner of Tridib's death, I do not have the words to give it a meaning. I do not have the words and I do not have the strength to listen". [228]

Urbashi Barat in her article, 'Imagination and Reality in *Shadow Lines*' has reflected upon grandmother's memory about Dhaka, about freedom that is absolutely appertaining. Grandmother assists the narrator to let his narrative keep on moving and thus readers get a glimpse of memories of the freedom struggle, the knotty and intricate relationship with Mayadebi, her affection for Jethamoshai which till date brought tears in her eyes and a smile on her lips, constitute the significant point for the novel at many places,

> "Over months she told me the house she had grown up in – Dhaka. In my grandmother's earliest memories her house was crowded ...... all the things people think about when they know that the best of their lives are already over". [125]

Her visit to Mayadebi in Calcutta made her so emotional that tears of joy and past memories mingled together and veiled her vision. Her narration of the upside down house often sent her into peels of laughter as they took her very close to Mayadebi again,

> "When the house was divided to frighten Maya I would make up the stories ..... But it's all gone now. They're all dead and I've nowhere to invent stories about and nowhere to escape to". [126]

Memories of Mayadebi never permit her to forget her uncle Jethamoshai left behind in Dhaka at the time of partition. She had a mission ahead to rescue her old uncle living alone in their family house. When she and Mayadebi reached Dhaka and saw their old house, reality took over memory,

> "Now my grandmother didn't know, where to look for. Suddenly the sights were falling into places like a stack of old photographs. The house edges were

> blurred but the shape of the outline was exactly as she remembered - large, welcoming and ungainly" [207]

The only living link with that old house washer uncle who did not remember anything of the present, nevertheless for him, the past was the only reality - the family, the profession of being a lawyer from which he was never able to separate his end in the riots. Urbashi Bharat's comments upon thus situation prove absolutely obvious that the memory of the past protected him, but the reality of the present killed him.

The novel is also remarkable for its impact of imagination and politics. The quest for the freedom of the protagonist and the other characters make this novel more contemporary. The idea of violence has been given a dual representation - a destructive one and a redemptive one.

Grandmother fondly re-lives her past in the atmosphere of riots and struggle. Her wish to do something for the people fighting for the freedom was sown to catch her dreams then, but she surely did it when the narrator remembered that she had given her most significant piece of jewelry for the same reason,

> "I gave it away to the fund for the war. I had to. For your sake; for your freedom. We have to wipe them out. We're fighting them properly with thanks, guns and bombs". [236]

Even though she is though a little crazy yet the spirit of freedom was dominant in it. The drops of blood flowing from her wound made her feel,

> "I must get to the hospital. I mustn't waste all this blood. I can donate it to the war front". [237]

The very issue of partition makes her angry though it has not taken place,

> "If there are no trenches or anything how're people to know? What's the difference then? And if there's

> no difference both sides will be the same. It'll be just like it used to be before, when we used to catch a train in Dhaka and get off in Calcutta without anybody stopping us. What was it all for then - partition, killing and everything if there's isn't something in between". [151]

Amitav Ghosh focuses on the political scenario i.e. the communal riots of 1964 in contrast to the joy and happiness for the same event,

> "On 27th Dec 63 two hundred and sixty years after it had been brought to Kashmir the sacred relic believed to be the hair of. Prophet Mohammed disappeared but also in Pakistan. But when it was recovered the city of Srinagar erupted with joy. People danced on the streets. But in Khulana a small town in Pakistan there was still a demonstration turned violent against the theft". [226]

The political upheaval that left the country totally shattered and destroyed by the partition, whose memory had left the narrator spellbound is expressed in dramatically -

> "the floor of the library dropping away under my feet leaving me suspended in space". [224]

The headlines of fifteen years old newspaper stating the facts of the riots made,

> "me begin my strangest journey; a voyage into a land outside space an expanse without distances, a land of looking glass events". [224]

The narrator throughout the novel struggles with silence,

> "It's not the silence of an imperfect memory. This silence lies outside the reach of the words. So complete is this silence that it took me fifteen years to discover that there was a connection between my nightmare

> bus ride and the events that befell Tridib and others in Dhaka .... I could not perceive that there was any connection between those events in Dhaka simply because Dhaka was in another country". [218-219]

Tridib falls a victim to the rioters crowd to save the life of May. Robi says,

> "When I look around I see May tiny with hundreds of men around her". [246]

Such a description catches the readers in the clutches of frenzy of political movements and gives a new direction to the thinking about the political situation,

> "Why don't they draw thousands of lines through the whole subcontinent and give every place a new name. The whole thing is a mirage. How can anyone divide a memory? If freedom were possible Tridib's death would have set me free ...... We stood a long time like that on the steps of that derelict Church in Clapham, three children of free state together clinging". [247]

The political scenario described so vividly in the *Shadow Lines* runs parallel to Khushwant Singh's novel *A Train to Pakistan*. The concept of freedom forms the focal point of both the novels. In *A Train to Pakistan*, Hindus are ready to lay down their lives to save the life of a Muslim priest, "Chacha, we'll not let anyone touch your hair". The same thoughts are spoken loudly in *Shadow Lines* where a Muslim is taking care of Jethamoshai and feels disturbed at the thought of his going away. Both these novels take readers into a contemplative mood. It forces then to muse over the aspects of politics which spreads its net of riots and bloodshed so widely that innocents have to pay for it with their lives. Both the novels raise the question about the cost of freedom, in which one has to pay to enjoy it. The peace disturbed in Mano majia is the same as the peace disturbed in Calcutta. The bloodshed found in *A Train to Pakistan* is the same as the bloodshed in the

Calcutta of *Shadow Lines*. Both these novels speak about the pains and pangs of partition.

The narrative texture giving the gist of memory is further created around the network of social relationships. The backlash of history often continues to haunt the characters, thereby inflicting them to present a comparative picture of past and present. Grandmother's memory pendulum comes handy in context,

> "Our house was quite a large house and my grandfather managed to keep the house together ...... Soon things came to a discussion. The brother even partitioned then father's nameplate". [123]

The relationship of grandmother and Mayadebi were often strengthened as the narrator remembers them,

> "Holding hands over my head like schoolgirls smiling with their lips pressed together full of merriment as though there was a mirror between them". [35]

The title *Shadow Lines* is apt. It has served the purpose of expressing the narrator's thoughts and thinking with so much of lucidity and clarity. At the very first glance, it is pronounced that it is by and large a *memory novel* where the 'shadows' of the past overhangs the present. There is continuously a tug-of-war between them. No character is ever able to detach himself from the past and present its identify to the present. It means, their identity is marred by the past. It unfolds new vistas for every character. All the deep buried secrets of the past present themselves nakedly to every character. Thus it helps them to construct a new future for themselves, which is more meaningful. Time is boundless and unending in this novel.

The story of the novel is of course one that quite obviously conforms the childhood of the narrator-protagonist and ending in his attaining adulthood and maturity. Each stage of his development is aptly demarcated through the change of location demanded of the bildungsroman. Thus, he moves consecutively from the Gole Park of the Calcutta of the fifties and sixties of his childhood, which corresponds to the countryside of the childhood of the traditional bildungsroman protagonist:

> "Gole Park was considered to be more or less outside Calcutta, in school when I said I lived there the boys from central Calcutta would often ask me if I caught a train every morning, as though I lived in some far-flung refugee camp on the border". [8]

He then goes to the more upper-class Southern Avenue house of adolescence, the place that sees the end of his childhood innocence through the way that his grandmother loses her iron control over herself and her son's family, the way, moreover, that he himself learns the meaning of fear and hate in the communal riot he observes, and experiences the painful awakenings of sexuality in his interactions and equations with May and Ila. Further, he lives in the greater world of college and Delhi, the Indian capital, which exposes him even more sharply to the realities of life. Finally, he goes to London, where his development is complete and from where he can return to India as a mature man, having bonded himself with his mentor and idol, Tridib, by his sexual union with Tridib's beloved, May, having learnt to cope, too, with his earlier traumas, and being thus prepared to face the world and the future. He is thus ready to return where he started from, India, and the novel ends, appropriately, with his plans to go home. Obviously, the even though does not foreground growing up as a move from country to town as the English bildungsroman usually does, it does present the widening and deepening of experience as a part of the process of maturing in terms of change of geographical location, while the titles of the two parts of the novel, 'Going Away' and 'Coming Home', reinforce the metaphor of movement, of the journey, which is the controlling metaphor of bildungsroman genre. The titles show the circularity of the development the novel presents, reinforced by the stories the narrator includes which impinge upon and parallel his own, so that the whole structure of the novel is like a collection of concentric circles or interconnected loops, like the ripples on the surface of a pond that continually move outward as he shifts spatially and temporally from the restricted world of the little flat in Gole Park through the wider circle of Southern Avenue. Then he goes to the provincial world of middle-class Calcutta to the centre of India, its capital, and finally to the centre of the colonial world and of the Commonwealth, the dream and the goal of the middle-class Bengali / Indian of his generation when he thinks of spreading his wings. It is appropriate, therefore, that it is in London that he completes his education, both formal and emotional, and from where he can return to India to begin a new life. The traditional bildungsroman ends with the attainment of experience and maturity. Ghosh ends with the prospect of a new beginning.

The Shadow Lines suggests that there are two major stages in individual development, marked by 'going away' and 'coming home', literally and metaphorically. The novel is in fact full of 'Going Aways' and 'Coming Homes', each journey impinging upon and paralleling the others, and thus extending its scope and its range. In the words of Suvir kaul –

> "In The Shadow Lines, it is of course the male narrator's growing imagination, empathy and emotionally which allow for the exploration and understanding of complex themes. As his horizons expand and become international in scope, his questions, memories and experiences provide the structure of the narrative. But even as his consciousness mediates and frames other voices, stories and experiences, we become aware that some of these voices counterpoint his narrative, and even interrogate his telling of the story .... In the many stories of this novel – overlapping at points, mismatched and contentious at others – The Shadow Lines becomes not simply a male bildungsroman, an

> authorized autobiography, with its obvious agenda and priorities, but also a dialogic, more open-ended telling of the difficulties, interdependencies and inequalities that compose any biography of a nation". [285-286]

The journey is central to The Shadow Lines. Indeed, it begins and ends with journeys, with one to England away from and India and with one to India from respectively. The last one may be the narrator's, but the first - foreshadowed, as it turns out by another one by an Englishman voyaging to India, a journey that, moreover, links three families, one British, two Indian, inextricably together - is undertaken not by the narrator himself but by his great-aunt and her family before he was born. This was a passage to England that would forever change the course of the narrator's life, for it was Tridib who had gone with his parents to London. This journey introduced Tridib not only to the infant May, but to an England ravaged by war and to experiences, his own as well as those of others, which opened up his imagination and his vision and helped him in turn to enlarge the emotional and intellectual world of the narrator, so that when the latter, too, 'goes away' to London he is in a sense also 'coming away'.

This kind of confusion between 'going away' and 'coming home' exists not only in the mind of the narrator's grandmother [152] but on other levels too, but it is only in the case of the narrator [and in Tridib's too] that it is sorted out. Thus, redoubtable Tha'mma had, as the wife of a railway engineer in Burma, led as peripatetic an existence as her sister, Mayadebi, was to do later as the wife of a diplomat, but, like her sister and brother-in-law, her travels mean little to her. She might live in "towns with fairy-tale names like Moulmein and Mandalay", but nothing in "that enchanted pagodaland" had seemed as real to her as its "railway stations and Bengalee colonies" [124], and her travels stopped when her husband died young. Now she was confined to a one-room tenement in Bhowanipore teaching in a school and bringing up her only son there, until he was old enough to find a job and move out to Gole Park. Many years later her great -niece Ila - whom she might deplore and even excoriate but who has as great a hold over the narrator's life as she has - travels all over the world with her parents, but can think of the exotic places she goes to as boringly similar, distinguished only by the location of the Ladies toilets in their airport lounges [20]. Subsequently, like Tha'mma,

> "although she had lived in many places, she had never travelled at all". [21]

like her great-aunt, Ila too, longs for freedom, but where for the younger woman freedom means an escape from the clutches of the past and the inhibitions they impose on her [88], for Tha'mma freedom is much more than being "left alone to do what [one] pleases" [89], it is something to be won through violence and bloodshed. In the end, because neither Tha'mma nor Ila knows what it is to travel, neither knows the meaning of freedom or selfhood, and both lead lives narrowed and unfulfilled and destructive for both themselves and for others.

It makes obvious that Tha'mma's journey to Dhaka, the place where she was born and lived until she married and from where she away and the home to which she returns to take away a senile uncle to what she now perceives as 'home', to "take [him] away from his past and thrust him into the future" [208]. Jethamoshai, nevertheless, cannot recognize the woman who has come home to take him home, and confidently says -

> "Once you start moving you never stop ...... I don't believe in this India - Shindia. It's all very well, you're going away now, but suppose when you get there they decide to draw another line somewhere? What will you do then? Where will you move to? .... As for me, I was born here, and I'll die here". [215]

For Jethamoshai who knows nothing of freedom and

nationhood, May is less foreign, more familiar, than a niece he has not set eyes on for several years and with whom he shares the most tenuous of emotional links. Tha'mma's attempt to free her uncle and take him on a homeward journey ends violently and sadly in three deaths, his own, the rickshaw-puller's and Tridib's. Even Illa's attempts to make a home for herself away from the India / Calcutta / Raibajar that would normally have been called her 'Home' are slashed by her own rigidity and lack of empathy, traits which she shares with her great-aunt. In the end, she destroys both Nick and herself and their hopes of happiness. Illa's journeys, later, are linear, and her development is therefore dubious. She finds the pains and the disillusionments of growing up, but never changes, never grows emotionally.

Tridib, on the other hand, has rejected his parents' life-style and is rooted in one place, but he is free than them or Ila. His imagination even soars farther and higher than anyone else's for it is –

> "a pure, painful and primitive desire, a longing for everything that was not in oneself, a torment of the flesh, that carried one beyond the limits of one's mind to other times and other places, and even, if one was lucky, to a place where there was no border between oneself and one's image in the mirror". [29]

This no doubt reflects the completion of selfhood through going beyond the self. That is why, Tridib can sacrifice himself, as no one else can. The ultimate journey, then, is the journey beyond the self. No wonder, then, that 'Going Away' ends in the Prices' house in London with the narrator left forlorn as Ila leaves him for Nick:

> "I knew that a part of my life as a human being had ceased; that I no longer existed, but as a chronicle" [112],

but 'Coming Home' ends with the narrator's union with May just before he leaves in India, a union that is not just sexual but a kind of spiritual rite of passage as well:

> "I could tell that she was glad, and I was glad too, and grateful, for the glimpse she had given me of a final redemptive mystery". [252]

May and Ila are significant figures in the narrator's development. They represent the two love affairs of sexual involvements of the bildungsroman. Interestingly, in the traditional Indian social ethic both would be regarded as unsuitable and unacceptable as sexual partners for the protagonist, May because she is Tridib's beloved [Tridib is after all his uncle; according to social norms], much older, and significantly, not even particularly sexually attractive even when she was young [11]. Ila herself as his cousin stands in the position of a sister, so the narrator's feelings towards her appear quite incestuous. According to the patriarchal norms of the male development plot both women should be unattainable. Both liaisons doomed. But both women help to mould the narrator's life and personality.

Ila is the first person to enter his life. If the narrator is Tha'mma's only grandchild, Ila is Tha'mma's sister's only grandchild, and as such they form a carefully contrasted couple:

> "it was said when we were children, that she and I were so alike that I could have been her twin – it was that very Ila who baffled me yet again with the mystery of difference". [31]

Ila occupies a position completely opposite to the narrator, enabling him to define himself through her. Where is bound to a strict and conventional middle-class upbringing in Calcutta, Ila leads an apparently exciting life abroad, visiting Calcutta only occasionally. But he has 'worlds to travel in' in is imagination, while she remains static and unimaginative [20]. He is culturally rooted in the soil of Bengal / India. But Ila has no roots and attempts to find herself in insignificant political activities in London and in a home by buying her a house and a reluctant husband. If Tha'mma had shown him the dangers and the emptiness of warped notions of nationalism, freedom and selfhood, Ila, the product of a colonialism in which the colonized rejects her past and her community and tries to internalize and participate in the world of the colonizer, reveals to him the hollowness of the world of the deracinated. Through Ila, then, the narrator learns to recognize the meaning of cultural dislocation and national identity. Even as a teenager, he can see through Ila's pretences and her need to cover up for her sufferings as an outsider in a society she longs to join but which will not accept her as much as the superficiality of her ideas of personal freedom and identity [89].

In brief, his interaction with Ila teaches him some harsh truths about emotional relationships. Like Pip with Estelle in *Great Expectations,* the narrator is often at Ila's mercy. When as a young boy, his mother tells Ila and her family how eagerly he had waited to see her, and Ila only smiles and shrugs, he feels deceived, for his mother -

> "had made public, then and forever, the inequality of our needs; she had given Ila the knowledge of her power and she had left me defenceless; naked, in the face that unthinkable, adult truth; that is not transitive, that one may need without oneself being needed". [44]

Ila deals with the narrator the way she does because to her he is the brother she never had [111], she is not insensitive or deliberately exploitative, but she makes him aware of his own sexuality and of his own response to contemporary sexual / gender mores, nevertheless. In the game of Houses played under the table of the cellar at Rajbajar he learns what the masculine role in family relationships is, and he experiences the first stirrings of the sexual urge when he sees her looked body there. When Tha'mma sees that his adolescent infatuation has developed into an adult passion she warns him that Ila is not better than a whore [89]. The truth, nevertheless, is very different. Ila is as much a victim of her husband and of the patriarchal world as Estelle was, and as chaste and virtuous:

> "Your see, you've never understood, you've always been taken in by the way I used to talk, when we were in college. I only talked like that to shock you, and because you seen to expect it of me somehow. I never did any of those things, I am about as chaste, in my own way, as any woman you'll ever meet". [188]

This shows that the narrator is in need to acquire his progress towards emotional maturity. Ila, then, is the nowhere woman, but she is certainly not like Tristran, Tridib's ideal lover, who transcends nationality [186]. She is a divided self, constantly trying to compensate for her weaknesses and unhappiness, and ultimately much worse off than he is.

The influence of May on the narrator's development is different but as important. As exotic as Ila, she is solidly a part of her own culture and shares none of Ila's anxieties and insecurities. She is the 'woman-across-the-seas' to Tridib's 'man without a country' [186], and the boy-narrator is infatuated with her as much as he is infatuated with Tridib and everything about Tridib, so that his feelings for her become a marker, as it were, of his self-identification with his mentor. In a sense, therefore, she stands in the way of his attainment of selfhood, though she is much more sympathetic and kindly than Ila. As the product of an alien culture, moreover, she cannot comprehend the realities of the Indian situation. The same moral earnestness and humanitarian impulse within her that are repelled by what the Victoria Memorial in Calcutta stands for making her ruthless and even destructive in her kindness. The young boy sees her force Tridib to kill a dying dog on the road to Diamond Harbour with a penknife, in a way that foreshadows Tridib's own death, for she forces Tridib to go to help Jethamoshai and Khalil in the middle of a rioting mob in Dhaka. Secure in the invulnerability of her position of an Englishwoman in an erstwhile colony, she refuses to acknowledge the certain danger that Tridib faces. Though the narrator admires and respects May, her honesty, her commitment and her obvious kindness, he had to understand that he must travel beyond her.

For him, however, May is a source of healing. She assists him when the young boy wants to go to Diamond Harbour with her and Tridib. She comforts him as an adult when Ila marries Nick, and though she repulses him when he tries to force himself upon her in a drunken state. She can perceive his feelings. At the end, he is about to return to India, she frees him from his emptiness and despair and re-links him to Tridib by explaining to him why for her Tridib's death was a sacrifice for the human values they both, and now the narrator too, upheld. By sleeping with him that night, she affirms his belief in and his identity with Tridib and affords him an insight into the spiritual nature of human relationships. This is what matures him in the end. He is prepared to receive his own adult role in society.

May's generosity, then, helps the narrator to accommodate himself to his world and to reconnect himself with the people he had left behind. This is a major theme of the Indian storytelling tradition in which there is ultimately a social feature. On the whole, the narrator of the novel is often aware his position and part in the continuing story of family relationships and national identity. His disillusionments, his pain, his triumph are as much those of his society as they are his own, so that his personal story becomes –

> "an extremely self-conscious meditation on the themes of nationality, internationality, cultural and historical self-determination, as also on the enormously conflicted transition from the temporary certitudes of

> the nationalist freedom struggle to the disillusions and discontents that have marked India as an independent state". [Suvir Kaul: 285]

Unlike the traditional protagonist, he is never alienated or estranged from his community. He never feels he must struggle on alone in a hostile or indifferent world. The mark of his adulthood is not his new ability to withstand alone the pressures of society in his perception of the meaning of existence, but, rather, the widening and deepening of his imaginative understanding of interpersonal and social relationships. The shadow lines between nations and cultures that the novel presents are, in fact, a metaphor for the shadowy divisions between people who have so much in common as to be almost the other's image. His new maturity enables the protagonist to accept and then to go above and beyond these divisions.

The mirrors that are so significant a trope in the novel emphasize this too. Mirrors are mode of self-recognition, as Lacan pointed out, but the novel itself constantly projects people, places and events as mirror images of each other, beginning with the boy narrator superimposing Tridib's image on to his own on the opening page itself and deciding that since he and Tridib are so much alike Tridib must look like him [3], and continuing its play of the double, postmodern fashion, throughout, its characters [the narrator and Ila, the narrator and Nick, Tha'mma and Ila, May and Mrs. Price, Nick and May, Snipe and Tridib, Alan and Nick, Ila and Francesca, Tresawen and Justice Datta-Chaudhuri, the two branches of the Bose family in Dhaka all mirror one another, as do its incidents and experiences, its cities and its neighbourhodds, as if to suggest that the lines that separate them - their lines of identity - are only shadows. Yet *The Shadow Lines* also insists that the individual must also go beyond the mirror image that denies separation, individuality through the use of the imagination, otherwise he or she will have to remain fixed on only one side of the mirror, static, constricted and one-dimensional, and therefore distorted and false. Recognition in a mirror is not enough to discover the self, and only the imagination can take one to the reality 'where there is no border between oneself and one's image in the mirror [29] and help us to see ourselves properly when it is used with precision [24], for it is only the imagination that enables us to invent ourselves –

> "We can not see without creating ourselves as unique individuals in the first place. The alternative to invention is not 'blankness' or a loss of identity; it is a false reality and a false identity. The truest identity can be treated and established through the power to invent that imagination alone has. Invention gives life and not a reflection; if we didn't try to create our own stories ourselves, we would never be free of other people's inventions". [31]

This, no doubt, is the ultimate and most significant test of the bildungsroman i.e. the selfhood it discovers should be genuine and self-created. Hence, the novel believes in the validity of this kind of selfhood as much as it believes in the significance of the mirror image.

On the whole, *The Shadow Lines* is a 'once upon a time' type of story narrated autobiographically yet with a multiple perspective, using memory as a source of recapturing fragments of the past. Though it begins at the beginning in the London of the 1939 war period and ends in the same London in 1979, it takes us back and forth in time and space, going away and returning home both geographically and intellectually. All the characters are often on the move, traveling all over the world, but they obtain real understanding and knowledge with their own experiences, their acquired experiences through imagination and then reliving the past linking it with the present realities. The journey-most is obviously established through the title of the two parts 'Going Away' and 'Returning Home'. They allude to first moving outward and then returning to the interior understanding and knowledge of the living forces of life. The past and the present are intricately woven with memory linking the events - not so much the exact happenings, as memory is bound to focus on certain aspects accurately and on certain in a blurred manner. The Narrator time and again emphasizes the techniques that memory plays:

> "I cannot remember when it happened or 'I don't know, I cannot tell [13]"

or referring to Tridib he says,

> "he didn't know whether it had really happened or he had imagined it" [144].

The novel begins in London of 1939 when Mayadebi, her husband and Tridib went to London. Tridib was about eight years old and May was just a kid. It ends in 1979 on the note of satisfaction of acquiring the knowledge of Tridib's death in 1964 and being free from guilt-consciousness for May, from nightmares about Tridib's murder for Robi and from ignorance about the mystery that surrounded Tridib's death for the Narrator-fifteen years of suffering and agony for both Robi and May and a puzzled and confused state of mind for the Narrator who must have been a child of eight at the time of Tridib's death in Dhaka. The suppressed truth about Tridib's death had hurt them all in one way or the other for Tridib's death is a constant presence in their lives. They travel through the fantasies of their past realities and arrive at the truth and the present realities of life. Ghosh utilizes the device of the folk-tale and fairy tale to relate the past to the present. The childhood memories of happenings and adulthood experiences of life, of 'heard things, imagined events and experiencing realities' are skillfully brought together by the shifting narration of the child Narrator and adult Narrator. The perspectives change and understanding follows.

Tridib is curious about his studying Ph.D. degree in Calcutta whereas the Narrator goes to London for his research degree. In London, the Narrator relieves in his imagination what Tridib had experienced in wartime London since Tridib had taught him to see accurately and vividly with his imagination. He follows the voyage of Tridib with his own microscopic memory and sharp imagination. Ghosh focuses on Tridib's experiences through the device of the parallel situation to project Tridib as the central and heroic figure in the life of all the characters, especially in the Narrator's life. In fact, the Narrator lives under the shadow of Tridib's stories, his knowledge, and his experiences. Only at the end of the novel does he step out of this shadow when he almost relives Tridib's life in the company of May.

Moving backward in time to the war-time London of 1939-40, the nameless Narrator [nameless, because he relives only what Tridib had described] describes in detail what Tridib the child of eight had observed. In a bomb-wrecked theatre he had seen two strangers - a man and a woman-coming together and making love. The woman is older than the man, Tridib could clearly observe. While growing up, he had kept up his relationship with May through letters and in one such letter in 1964, he writes to her about the strangers' love-making with May in a ruined place. It is May who tells the Narrator of her response to them and her journey to the Calcutta of 1964. The third such situation is portrayed when May and the Narrator lie together in London in 1979, on the eve of the Narrator's return to India. All the three situations are presented specifically after violent happenings, in War-torn London, riot-affected Calcutta and again in London after remembering and recreating Tridib's death in riot-affected Dhaka. Ghosh portrays violence-affected far-off places both in Time and Space only to give meaning to love-making-the reality of life-force and to show how Tridib, May and the Narrator grow mature in understanding and attain redemption through Love. The situations are the same, but the players are different. Both May and the Narrator find release from the mystery of Tridib's death, a sacrificial offering as May calls it, which cannot be explained or understood:

> "He gave himself up; it was a sacrifice. I know I cannot understand it. I know I mustn't try, for any real sacrifice is a mystery." [252]

and the Narrator too feels grateful.

> "for the glimpse she had given me of a final redemptive mystery." [252]

Ghosh presents Tridib's death as a mystery, which, in fact, historically speaking is not a mystery, nor a sacrifice, since Ghosh presents a similar event in Calcutta before May and Tridib leave for Dhaka. It is a stray dog that is put to peaceful death by May with the help of Tridib. What she could do with the dog, she is unable to do with Jethamoshai and Tridib. They die a dog's death. Through this parallel and yet contrasting event the novelist focuses on the killings, accidental and deliberate. Tridib had helped May to put the dog to rest:

> "Then Tridib lunged at it [the dog] gripped its neck and head firmly with both hands and pinned it to the tarmac ..... May leant forward .... Then she flicked the penknife open with her thumbs .... May made a final, determined jab with the penknife and sprang back ..... Its twisted body twitched convulsively and then it lay still". [173]

Tridib believes that she had done the right thing and relieved the dog of the painful suffering. He wants her to do the same thing to him if so required.

"Promise me, he said, that you'll do it for me too, if I should ever need it". [174]

May bears guilty feeling for seventeen years about the death of Tridib who is killed by the mob in Dhaka. There Tridib had followed her, but though he could protect May, he could not save Jethamoshai and Khalil, May feels that she would not have been hurt by the mob as she was an English lady. It is a painful memory for her and she tries to suppress it deep in her heart. But at the time she thought that it was as simple as cutting short the painful suffering of the dog, to help Jethamoshai and Khalil the cycle rickshawman, and save them from the violent mob.

> "..... I didn't know what I was doing, and I'd get everyone killed. I didn't listen; I was a heroine. I wasn't going to listen to a stupid, cowardly woman. But she knew what was going to happen. Everyone there did, except me. I was the only one who didn't". [250]

With this confession of May, Ghosh projects Tridib as the heroic persona. May stupid to think of saving people from the mindless violent mob, there does not seem to be any mystery about Tridib's death, nor does it prove a convincing sacrifice. As is pointed by Rajeshwari Rajan–

> "It is an ending that has a false ring of a sentimental resolution". [298]

For May who had seen Tridib running towards the mob and then being dragged in:

> "He vanished. They had cut Tridib's throat, from ear to ear". [251]

It is an act of sacrifice. Talking it over to the Narrator after seventeen years of guilt-consciousness. May is bound to feel a release from it. To the western mind of May, Tridib's death is a mysterious sacrifice. What the Narrator feels about this is not revealed. The three situations of love-making in the London of 1939, in the Calcutta of 1964 and again in the London of 1979 are presented with a view to give meaning to love in life even against the violent historical events. The Narrator relives Tridib's story of 1939 and May's story of 1964 in 1979 through his imagination. These stories told through different perspectives of what the child, Tridib had observed and mature May had experienced, merges with the Narrator's present and are likely to guide him and May in future. For him, it is arriving at an understanding of the May-

Tridib relationship as also his own relationship with May and Ila.

Ghosh has portrayed the Narrator's relationship with Ila using the device of parallel situations. It is a game of House played by Ila and Nick in London and Ila and the Narrator in Calcutta. The Narrator remembers Ila in Raibajar:

> "It is the other eight years old Ila and I, my own other - both of us sitting under that table in Raibajar and she is crying because she had just finished telling me the story of Nick Price and Magda". [181]

Then she was crying and now also in 1979, she is crying sitting with the narrator in the cellar. It is the story of betrayal on both the occasions. Once again it is May who tells the story of Ila's childhood betrayal. While returning from school, Nick had deserted Ila when she was trapped by the white students of her class only because she had proved herself cleverer than them in the class room, though Ila keeps up the illusion of her rescue by Nick when she tells the Narrator about Magda's rescue by Nick. Now when she is married to him she feels betrayed by Nick as he has affairs with other women. But Ila wants to live in the make-believe world of illusion, of loyalty and love between them. Ila knows about Nick's weakness but her love for him and her love for herself do not permit her to accept the realities of life. In this game of House, the Narrator often feels the presence of Nick in his childhood and now in his present life. Nick is a mirror-image in his life. His efforts at objective-effacement by reducing himself and Nick to mere mirror-images is thwarted. Ila who is often on the move and yet never rooted in any geographical place yearns for freedom from the bonds of culture and tradition. She longs for a house of her own to be a home, but what she gets is simply a house gifted by her father. She neither attains real freedom nor does she acquire the home she loves so much. It remains merely a game for her and Nick. The

Narrator is a rejected lover, but finds solace in the company of May for a single night in London on the eve of his departure, his return to his homeland.

Though Tridib is visualized as a heroic person in the Narrator's life and remains a constant presence, it is more or less through memories that he is recreated. The Narrator lives almost all his life under the shadow of Tridib's stories. But through these stories and his memories, through this maze of life, the Narrator-protagonist emerges a wiser person. He begins to understand that there is another world independent of his imagined-past world, outside the time frame of the past. There is his own world of realities and experiences. It appears that he begins to understand this world of his and to realize how the fragments of the past memories help him to accept the new path of life. The novel points to the future for him, unhampered by the shadows of the past. In A. N. Kaul's words –

> "The frequent time-switches in the novel underline a process whereby the narration of the real or imagined past of one person takes hold of the imagination of another and prepares the way for his own encounter with the same reality in the future. Future experience is thus contained, viz memory, in past narration and, as in the case of reality and imagination, the novel leaves little doubt as to which of the two, in terms of a vivid and meaningful experience, is the more 'real'. [308]

Though novel appears to be more about historical events and violent happenings, partition and border-lines, dividing the nations, in fact it is more about people who act on their life against these problems, acquire a clear understanding, and accept the realities of lines, but find that in their personal lives, lines are blurred and shadows must be discarded. Unlike Khushwant Singh's *Train to Pakistan, The Shadow Lines* examines the effect of borders on the personal lives, long after Partition and establishes Ghosh as a major voice after Rushdie.

In a nutshell, *The Shadow Lines* is a complex work of art, and as such suggests a number of themes and ideas. Different critics have interpreted it in different ways. To Blackstone, its dominant themes are [a] love, married life and family, and [b] self-shedding and self-dramatization. According to David Diaches, the main theme the late fiction is the relation of personality, death and time to each other, the relation of the individual to sum of experience in general. According to others its theme is the contrast between the rational and logical approach and the emotional and intuitive approach to the problems of life, According to Norman Friedman, the novel studies subject and object and the nature of reality. In other words, the novel examines the relationship of one person to another; the relation of man to nature; and the relation of art to life. In the end, we find that the novel exercises strange fascination upon its readers. The novel obviously is incredibly rich in its story and theme. It is packed with thought, with emotion, and with integrated and elaborate imagery. It is a living whole and such a whole, though bearing upon it no mark of efforts could not have been brought forth without great labour.

WORKS CITED

Dixon, Rovert. "Travelling in the West: The Writing of Amitav Ghosh", *The Journal of Commonwealth Literature,* 31.1,1996.

Menon, Ritu and Kamla Bhasin, 'Recovery, Rupture, Resistance: Indian State and Abduction of Women During Partition,' in *Economic and Political Weekly,* 28, no. 17 [April 24, 1993].

Blackstone, Bernard. *Amitav Ghosh – A Commentary,* London, 1999.

Barat, Urbashi, "Imagination and Reality" in *The Shadow Lines.* Delhi: Prestige Books, 1999.

Kaul, Suvir. "Separation Anxiety : Growing Up Inter/ National in *The Shadow Lines*. In Ghosh 268-286.

Rajan, Rajeshwari. *The Division of Experience in The Shadow Lines,* from Amitav Ghosh's *The Shadow Lines,* Delhi: OUP, 1995.

Kaul, A. N. *A Reading of The Shadow Lines,* from Amitav Ghosh's *The Shadow Lines,* Delhi: OUP, 1995.

4

In An Antique Land

Ghosh's third book, *In an Antique Land* [1992] straddles the generic borderlines between fact, fiction, autobiography, history, anthropology, and travel book. Ghosh maps ethnographic fieldwork undertaken in the Egyptian villages of Lataifa and Nashawy onto his subsequent research into medieval Indian Ocean trade. In so doing he explores the connections and ruptures between two worlds, the medieval and the contemporary. As the book progresses the two seemingly disparate strands of the Egyptian families and village communities with whom Ghosh resides in the early 1980s, and the narrative of his attempts to trace 'the slave of MS. H.6' increasingly dovetail, each narrative helping to shed light on the other.

Ghosh parodies and subverts the traditional ethnographic trope of confining personal commentary to prefaces or afterwards. He chooses to omit the conventional arrival scene, and his description of the Egyptian village begins with the narrator already settled, somewhat unhappily, at the house of Abu-'Ali. Whereas much classic ethnography begin with an introduction describing the sense of strangeness felt by the ethnographer on arrival at the field site, and then banish personal observation from the main body of the text, Ghosh makes no mention of his arrival, though his feelings of alienation and the curiosity his presence provokes are emphasized throughout. Ghosh too sandwiches his text between a 'Prologue' and an 'Epilogue', but it is worth noting that these are more novelistic terms than the scholarly 'Preface' or 'Afterword', immediately indicating the text's imaginative purchase on anthropology.

In an Antique Land is a brilliant hybrid, a subversive history in the guise of a traveller's tale. It tells the story of two Indians in Egypt. The first was a twelfth-century slave; the second is Amitav Ghosh, who stumbled upon the slave in the margins of letters that were written by the slave's master. His curiosity piqued - even ill defined, the slave's presence in the records of medieval history was completely out of the ordinary - Ghosh journeyed to Egypt in 1980 to try to fill in the details of the slave's life. His search - which would last for ten years - began in a tiny village two hours from Alexandria where Ghosh found himself among people for whom 'the world outside was still replete with wonders of the unknown.' There was Abu-Ali, his gargantuan landlord; Khamees the Rat, the beady-eyed local wit; his adversary, the Imam; Zaghloul the weaver [once so obsessed with a girl that he spent his nights kneeling outside her window to listen to the sound of her breathing]; and young, quiet Nabeel, who would be left stranded in Baghdad at the outset of the Gulf War.

These were zealous Muslims who found him, a Hindu, fascinating but utterly incomprehensible. Yet they willingly became his guides as he sifted through fact and conjecture, piecing together the slave's journey from India to Egypt. Ghosh discovered an 'elusive and mysterious acquaintance' in the slave, with whom he seemed to share, across eight hundred years, the experience of dislocation, and who seemed to have given him 'a right to be there, a sense of entitlement.' And, moving between the present and the ancient past, between his own life and the slave's, Ghosh creates an exuberant multi-layered narrative, rich in detail and anecdote, that affords us not only an inkling of the slave's life, but also a unique understanding of the private life of the world that both he and the author came to inhabit.

The past, as the English novelist L.P. Hartley once observed,

> "is another country. They do things differently there."

How much more different must the past appear when it is sited literally in another country, especially such a country as Egypt, where the past intrudes so insistently into the contemporary world, and where everyday life is a wondrous amalgam of successive civilizations and both their glories and discontents. Such is the underlying motif of *In An Antique Land,* Amitav Ghosh's fascinating study which blends a historical detective story with his own experiences as a young Indian graduate student in the small Egyptian village of Lataifa, a few miles [and several centuries] outside the city of Alexandria.

In the 1980's, while enrolled as a graduate student in cultural anthropology at the University of Alexandria, Ghosh learned of the discovery in a Cairo synagogue of a cache of ancient manuscripts, some of them dating from the 12th century AD. The collection included letters from a Jewish trader who owned an Indian slave - a fact both intriguing and unsettling. Ghosh became first interested, then obsessed, with this minor historical mystery, and in his search for answers found himself drawn into the daily lives of two other outsiders, the Jewish merchant and his Indian slave in medieval Muslim Egypt. At the same time, and with equal mixture of mystery and fascination, Ghosh attempts to understand, and be understood by, the residents of Lataifa, who remain, in many ways, inhabitants of that other country, the past.

Ghosh writes with grace, lucidity, and clear-eyed perception. His Lataifa is a real place, whose residents are all individuals and who are portrayed, regardless of their status or character, not with condescension but with a high degree of respect and even affection. His growing acceptance into village life is marked by unexpected bursts of humor, much of it provided by the misunderstandings that occurs at the edges of cultural interaction, and by sobering reality, as when young men leave the only home they have ever known for the dangers of life in Iraq, then trembling on the brink of war with the West.

Ghosh accomplishes his interweaving of past and present with remarkable skill and agility, and his account should please the general reader as well as those interested in Middle Eastern and Jewish history, or contemporary village life in one of the region's most important nations. In the end, Ghosh realizes more than a passing resemblance to his 12th century countryman, and comes to appreciate and understand, to a greater degree, the lives of Lataifa and its people.

Amitav Ghosh's *In An Antique Land* shows the repossessing of historical experience, which reclaims the past. The novel unfolds the story of two Indians in Egypt, and Abraham Ben Yiju, a Jewish merchant originally from Tunisia who came to India around A. D. 11130. Ben Yiju, who lived in India from seventeen years, married a Nair woman, acquired an Indian 'slave', Bomma, a native of Tulunad. Bomma was with his master when he went back to Egypt in the last years of his life. The other Indian in Egypt is Amitav Ghosh, who in 1980, went there to trace the story of Bomma. His search, which was last more than ten years, began in a small village, two hours South of Alexandria. His guides in the village were his neighbours: Abu Ali, his landlord; Khamees the Rat, the beady eyed local wit; his adversary, the Imam; Zaghloul the weaver and the quiet Nabeel whose personal fate-left stranded in Baghdad at the outset of the Gulf War – bespeaks a larger one for Egypt and the 'developing World'.

The novel gives the subversive history in the guise of a traveller's tale. At the outset, the writer makes it clear that he plans to do research leading towards a doctorate in Social Anthropology. He went to Egypt to trace the history of the slave of MS H.6. The reader finds himself transported to Lataifa and Nashawy with the river. The reader too experiences the journey and gets interested and absorbed in Ghosh's tale of his experiences and findings in a new country. The alien culture, customs, religion, social life etc. leave an impact on the minds of the readers, as much it leaves on Ghosh's mind. The tale is packed with anecdotes and exuberant details, it provides magical, intimate insights into Egypt from the Crusades to Operation Desert Storm. For example, Ustaz Sabry's account of war between Iran and Iraq gives the reader a feel of what it has done to the people –

> "It's we who've been the real gainers in the war', he told me. The rich Arab countries were paying the Iraqis to break the back of the Islamic Revolution in Iran. For them, it was a matter of survival, of keeping themselves in power. And in the meantime, while others were taking advantage of the war to make money, it was the Iraqis who were dying on the front". [321]

As mentioned before, the author's guides, in the guise of locals, often had a tale to narrate to him to familiarize him with the people and the area. Therefore,. in such a case the reader encounters a story within a story at several places in the novel. This technique increases the validity of an event or a story and provides a shift in the ongoing tale, which in turn provides a change to the reader. The reader also hears the story along with the writer. For instance, the story of the government to pass the canal through that grave etc. is a miracle story. The readers, though unbelievable, believe the story. There is no interference of any kind from the author and so one does not doubt its originality.

The story is narrated in the third person and is divided into six sections – Prologue, Lataifa, Nashawy, Mangalore, Going Back and Epilogue. The reader so travels to each of these places in these sections along with the author. The two stories, that of the writer's encounters with Egyptian people and tracing of slave Bomma, go hand in hand throughout the novel. Within these sections, a section follows each sub section of Lataifa or Nashawy on Ghosh's visit to Cairo to do his research. The reader is listening to two tales simultaneously. It will not be an exaggeration if one says that the reader goes through the whole process of research if one says that the reader goes through the whole process of research in anthropology as Ghosh puts his research data in the form of a tale. Ghosh has made the tale lively and vivid by adding touches of humour while describing his characters -

> "Every now and again, Abu Ali would ..... send his wife into fetch his best dark glasses, and shout for the moped to be wheeled out into the courtyard. He would hitch up the hem of his jallabeyya and then, lifting up his leg, he would mount the vehicle with a little sidelong hop, while his son held it steady ...... he would go shooting off down the road, his jallabeyya ballooning out around him, while the moped, in profile, diminished into a thin, sharp line - it was like watching a gargantuan lollipop being carried away by its stick". [28]

Ghosh introduces his characters also by beginning a new tale about each of them. During the course of this tale, the characters are introduced, their character is built and they are then allowed to narrate another story about their family or village. This helps the author in establishing them as true characters. Isma'il and Nabeel are introduced to the readers in a story in which the author remembers how he had first met the two of them. Memory plays a significant role in narrating this tale of an antique land, as it does in the other novels of Ghosh. The reader almost re-lives the experiences of Ghosh through his memory and narration. The ease with which he moves from one story to another is amazing. One comes across a variety of people residing in villages in Egypt and cannot help comparing them with the people residing in Indian villages. Third person narration is never free from a bias or likes and dislikes of the author. Ghosh, too, develops a liking for Nabeel and Isma'il during the course of the novel. Nevertheless, an objective view of the details regarding the curiosity of Egyptians about Indian Customs, burning of the dead, circumcision of sex organ etc. compensates for any bias. There can be a tendency on the part of the author to protect one's country or to present it in a better light, which Ghosh abstains from doing.

Within this tale of a distant land, Ghosh seeks the opportunity to narrate the tale of his land also i.e. Calcutta and the formation of East Pakistan. This political event had left a deep impact on the author's memory, which he never fails to share with his readers at some point in his novels. The stories of riots are often the same anywhere in the world. Ghosh's sensitivity to such situations can be felt when he says –

> "The fact was that despite the occasional storms and turbulence their [Nabeel's] country had seen, despite even the wars that some of them had fought in, theirs was a world that was far more gentler, far less violent, very much more humane and innocent than mine". [210]

By pondering over such issues, Ghosh's tale touches certain universal issues and rises above the art of mere story telling.

Ghosh has a superb sense of history, geography and anthropology. For instance, he spends almost seven to eight pages describing Caro, how it got its name, its geography, its history etc. acquainting the reader with the place. The tale is very formative, be it, the Crusade, War between Iran and Iraq, fear of Saddam Hussein, Iraqi invasion of Kuwait etc. from the point of view of political happenings in that country. Similarly, the reader relives the history of the geographical location of Mangalore as a port, its neighbouring ports, the trade carried out then, language spoken in Mangalore, Nairs in Kerala, Vaniyas of Gujarat who settled there, rulers ruling at the time Ben Yiju resided in India etc. The medieval heritage of Manglore comes alive in the vivid description of the place given by the writer. Ghosh's knowledge of Arabic language and Tulu is also really admirable.

Ghosh proves himself to be a true anthropologist as he unravels one truth after another with a new story. In the east, hundred pages or so of the novel, history has been translated into fiction to trace Ben Yiji's journey and Bomma's origins and what happened to him. Each historical detail has been documented with the true sincerity that leads us to Ghosh's completion of his research work, which he mentioned at the outset. In his quest for Bomma's origins and life, the reader notices Ghosh's scholarly knowledge of religion e.g. Judaism, Islam, Hinduism or Sufism. The reader witnesses a fusion of fiction and history by a traveler who makes his tale authentic and true by doing so.

Ghosh's narrative accomplishment in his four novels has won him praise and recognition from his readers. He makes efforts to get new technique, that of story telling through the use of memory, a craft quite simple, and achieves a total effect on the readers. He carefully narrates each story, builds up and holds the attention of the reader, and moves with a steady direction towards his final end. The reader too gets involved and interested in this anthropological research. The novel also offers vivid glimpses of the many small, indistinguishable, intertwined histories - Indian and Egyptian, Muslim and Jewish, Hindu and Muslim - which prevailed until some countries ago, but which then become partitioned in several areas where they had one existed. The novel, nevertheless, works richly with the task Ghosh suggests. He has created a novel which is beautiful and powerful, but also works to record and reclaim history, history which like Ustaz Sabry's name enlightens, and like Bomma's point the way to an understanding of the past, which can lead to a more fruitful reckoning with the present and the future.

In An Antique Land is obviously a travelogue, but underneath lies Ghosh's minute discussion of the problems that his characters face due to migration. The story revolves around the research being conducted by the narrator Amitav, in the field of social anthropology. The discussion begins in the 12th century and ends in the year 1991, at the commencement of the Gulf War, popularly known as Operation Desert Storm. This research exposes Amitav to the social structure in Egypt.

The theme of migration leading to alienation is elaborated in the characters of Ben Yiju, who in the very beginning the novel is described as -

> "A Jewish merchant, originally of Tunisia, who had gone to India by way of Egypt, as a trader, and had spent seventeen years there. A man of many accomplishments, a distinguished calligrapher, scholar and poet, Ben Yiju had returned to Egypt having amassed great wealth in India". [19]

Ben Yiju has successfully established his trade in India with the help of his mentor Madam Ibn Bundar, a trader in Aden, Egypt. Young Ben Yiju has arrived in Aden with dreams in his eyes, but had to leave for India under mysterious circumstances and this is revealed in one of Madman's letters, wherein there is a shaded reference to these circumstances. The narrator describes this letter and its contents as -

> "Despite its brevity and the suddenness of its termination, there is one fact the passage does serve to establish beyond any doubt. It proves that Ben Yiju's departure for India was not entirely voluntary, that something had happened in Aden that made it difficult for him to remain there or to return". [161]

Ben Yiju's marriage to Ashu and also his inability to integrate with the people of India can be understood in this light. He must have decided to marry an Indian girl only because it was impossible for him to return to Egypt in the near future. The sense of being a fugitive must have created a huge hurdle for Ben Yiju in accepting India as his home. The guilt of wrong-doing must have haunted him during his entire stay in India. He remained in India as an 'Outsider' because he was acutely aware of his own distinct identity, that of a Jew who belonged to Egypt. Ben Yiju was able to relate to those Muslim Arab traders who like him had settled in Mangalore, as they spoke the same language, shared the same dress code and belonged to the same continent -

> "Ben Yiju's closest affiliations in Mangalore would of course have lain with the community with which he shared his taste in food and clothing: the expatriate Muslim Arabs who were residents in this city - indeed for most purposes he would have counted himself as one of them". [279]

Ben Yiju must have felt more grounded in their presence, because they were like the various branches of the same tree, which had its roots in the Middle-East.

Ben Yiju must have left Aden in such a haste, that it must have been difficult for him to contact his family in Ifriqya situated in the Mediterranean port of Mahdia. And then for years, he lived the life of a fugitive in a faraway land making it difficult for him to keep in touch with his family back home. And then one fine day, he received some news of his brother Mubashir, which makes him think about 'Going Back':

> 'IT WAS PROBABLY in the mind 1140s or so that Ben Yiju began to think seriously of returning to the Middle East. At about that time, after many years of silence, he finally received news about a member of his family, his younger brother Mubashir, who as far as he knew was still living in their homeland Ifriqiya". [299]

As soon as Ben Yiju comes to know about the hardship that his family has faced at the hands of natural disasters and due to attacks by the Sicilian army, he immediately decides to return. He had been planning his return for a long time but,

> "This time Ben Yiju did do it: a year later in 1149, he was back in Aden, with all his worldly goods and his two adolescent children". [302]

The extent of Ben Yiju's alienation is evident from his over-zealous response at the news of his long-lost family. The long separation had not dried up his feelings, but had in fact increased his longing for his family in Egypt. The letter that he writes to his brothers immediately after retuning from India illuminates the depth of his anguish at being separated from his family and homeland:

> "On 11 September 1149, Ben Yiju wrote his brother a long letter from Aden. His return had stirred many long-settled memories, and he was now overcome with a desire to reclaim his family and the remembered landscapes of his childhood: 'I do not know what to write', the letter begins, 'so strong is my longing and so ardent my yearning". [302]

Thus, Ghosh has been successful in brining out the feeling of alienation and loneliness experienced by Ben Yiju in the 12th century. Through this Ghosh has once again managed to prove the theory that migration does create the problem of alienation. This story of the 12th century is once again recreated in the 20th century, with minor changes in characters and place. In the 20th century, it is Nabeel who is at the centre of the story.

Nabeel is a very contemporary character. He represents the youth of the third World developing countries who are hypnotized by the dream of success, and are eager to go to any extent to achieve this success. Nabeel and Ismail are introduced as two young students, whom the narrator meets when he is in Nashawy, Egypt. Both these young men have a burning passion to become officers in the village co-operative, a post which was held in high-esteem in their small town of uneducated Fellaheen community.

Out of these two boys, Nabeel is more passionate about achieving success in life. Nabeel's childhood has been spent in acute poverty, and it considered his father responsible for this poverty, because of his low-paying job of a watchman. He desired to have a white-collar, well-paying job in order to improve his lot, and also to improve their standing among other rich relatives –

> "Nabeel, on other hand, hated his family's poverty and loyal though he was to his father, he considered a watchman's job demeaning, unworthy of his lineage. He had always been treated as a poor relative by his more prosperous Badawy cousins, and he had responded by withdrawing into the defensive stillness of introspection". [150]

Nabeel and Ismail are allured by the prospects of fast money. They are carried away by the promises offered by the developed and economically powerful countries. Both of them leave their homeland and move to Iraq in search of better economic prospects. And materially speaking they do attain this success. Ismail works as a construction labourer and Nabeel works as an assistant in a photographer's store. Though their jobs are not highly respectable, they are able to earn a lot more than what they would have earned his family in Egypt as officers in the co-operative. Nabeel is able to relieve his family from its downtrodden state, and is also able to fulfill his family's dreams of acquiring material comforts –

> "Later Nabeel had sent money for a television set and a washing – machine and then, one day, on one of his tapes he had talked about building a new house. Those tumble down old rooms they'd always lived in wouldn't last much longer, he'd said, he would

> be glad to have a new house ready, when he came back to Egypt". [319]

Nabeel like many other young men of Nashawy had gone to work 'outside', for a short time, just to ear enough. But who will decide when it is enough. Gradually, the material success assumes the form of bog, which makes these young men its captive and they find it difficult to relinquish its magic. Nashawy was slowly turning into another 17th century English countryside town, with all its youth and its power migrating to the countries rendering greater economic success. The narrator is able to make this connection, as soon as he visits Egypt after a gap of eight years -

> "I could not have begun to imagine a change on this scale when I left Nashawy in 1981; revisiting it now, a little less than eight years later, it looked as those the village had been drawn on to the fringers of a revolution - except that this one had happened in another country, far away". [321]

By completing this budding revolution in Nashawy to 17th century England, Ghosh is trying to draw a parallel between the two at many levels. One of them is about the conflict between an individual's emotional happiness versus his market value, i. e. his capacity to earn. An individual acquires his significance within his family only after he begins to earn substantially, and then onwards he is viewed only in the light of his pay-packet. Nabeel lands into this trap the moment, he decides to go and work 'outside' - in Iraq. Nabeel loses his standing within the family as a living emotional human-being, and becomes a money-producing machine. When Amitav inquires with Nabeel's family about his life in Iraq, they try to discourage his inquisitiveness -

> "What are things like in Iraq?" I asked Fawzia. "Does Nabeel like it there?" She nodded cheerfully. He was very happy, she said; in his tapes he always said he

> was doing well and that everything was fine". [321-322]

The narrator is stupefied at this casual reply, but is more troubled at Ali, Nabeel's brother's response, because even he gives a very detached answer to the question posed by the narrator about Nabeel's well being, Ali shrugged, as far as he knew', he said, 'Nabeel was well enough'.

Nabeel's sister-in-law's immediate response to this confirms out fear about the value of Nabeel's existence. She says 'And besides' said Fawzia, 'What would Nabeel do back here? Look at Ismai'l just sitting at home, no job, nothing to do" [351]. Fawzia does not consider Nabeel's discomfort, his loneliness and his pain of separation, while counting the money that he sends from Iraq. Nabeel's safe and sound return is neither hers nor her family's first priority. While on the other hand, Isma'l, who has had a first hand experience of the terrors they faced in Iraq, and is also aware of the mental and physical toll that it takes on these immigrants, and so he once again emphatically adds,

> "But still, he wanted to come back, He's been there three years. It is more than most and it's aged him you have seen, what I mean if you saw him. He looks much older. Life is not easy out there". [352]

Nabeel is especially burdened by this sense of alienation because he is shown to be more sensitive and considerable than the other men of this age. He treasures familial bonding, and that is why he was able to understand the loneliness that the narrator experiences during his stay in Egypt. And it is this incident which immediately strikes the narrator, as soon as he is told about Nabeel's being alone to face the war in Iraq, as most of his friends and relatives have returned to Egypt -

> My mind went back to that evening when I first met Nabeel and Isma'il: how Nabeel had said: 'It must

> make you think all the people you left at home when you put that kettle on the stove with just enough water for yourself. It was hard to think Nabeel alone, in a city headed for destruction". [353]

Nabeel's pathetic story ends on a very sad, pessimistic note by the narrator suggesting his complete annihilation in the world of History. In brief, we are known to the fact that the roots of man's alienation are found in the life of Nabeel. Ghosh has been successful, and in the bargain the roots invite alienation. Ghosh has been successful in portraying man's loneliness and helplessness against the strong force of human nature.

WORKS CITED

Ghosh, Amitav. 1992. *In An Antique Land,* New Delhi: Ravi Dayal Publisher.

www.ajax prenhall.com. http://www.ajax.prenhall.com

www.anothersucontinent.com.http://www.anothersubcontinent.com/forums/index.php?showtopic=1868

www.answers.com.http://www.answers.com/main/ntquery?method=4&dsname=Wikipedia+Images&dekey=Anita_Desai.jpg&gwp=8

www.new.bbc.co.uk.http://new.bbc.co.uk/2/hi/entertainment/6745609.stm.

5

The Calcutta Chrosome

Amitav Ghosh's *The Calcutta Chromosome,* spans one century and three continents, and the main characters are an Egyptian data analyst and a malaria obsessed Indian living in New York City. Its part science fiction, part history, part thriller, part detective story. Certain chapters are reminiscent of Dickens or Poe, while others feel like something out of "The X-Files," It's an ambitious, often entertaining novel that addresses, with mixed success, big questions about history, science, knowledge and identity. The novel is framed by the story of Antar, a lonely, law level, overworked Egyptian data analyst, and Murugan, his Indian colleague. Murugan has a strange theory about Ronald Ross, the Nobel Laureate who discovered how mosquitoes transmit malaria; that someone "had systematically interfered with Ronald Ross's experiments to push malaria research in certain directions while leading it away from others." This "bizarre hypothesis" leads to Murugan's disappearance in Kolkatta on World Mosquito Day, August 20,1995 years later, in a near future New York City, Murugan's I. D. Card is discovered by Antar's personable computer, Ava. For reasons that are never adequately explained, Antar decides to investigate Murugan's disappearance and his "other Mind" theory that Ross was a pawn in someone else's malaria research project.

Nothing in this novel stands still for very long. The narrative soon leaves Antar and moves on rapidly from place to place, traveling and mutating like one of the malaria parasites at the heart of this story. We see Kolkatta in 1995, where Murugan meets Urmila Roy, a journalist struggling with conflicting demands of career and family; a military hospital in Secunderabad in 1895 where Ross is beginning his malaria research, and where two uneducated servants, Lutchman and Mangala, know more than they should about the malaria Parasite; an abandoned train station in Renupur where the writer Phulboni spends a horrific night that will inspire a collection of allegorical stories; a village in Egypt where, as a child, Antar watches an old Hungarian archaeologist sift the sand with tweezers.

These seemingly disparate episodes Cohere to expose a bewildering world in which none of the ordinary rules of science or logic apply. An alternative history of malaria research beings to emerge, in which a tem working in India in the late 1880s discovers that the malaria parasite can be used to transfer a lot more than just malaria from person to person. Soon it's impossible to know what's true, or who. It seems that Antar, Murugan, Urmila and Phulboni are all caught up in this counter-science project, but they don't know exactly how. No one can ever really know, explains Murugan, because "to know something is to change it, therefore in knowing something you've already changed what you think you know so you don't really know it at all; you only know its history".

There are occasional moments of vivid writing, as when Phulboni sees, through a train window, "The stillwaters, lying in great silver sheets under the lowering monsoon skies." In his writing, Ghosh displays a talent for finding vivid details and symbols, a description of a stand of rubber trees, or a young girl dancing at a wedding, that develop his ideas. In *The Calcutta Chromosome,* ideas aren't conveyed with this kind of imaginative force. Murugan explains his theories to Antar and Urmila in long, awkward dialogue passages that interrupt rather than impel the pace of the Story.

Ghosh imagines the science of malaria, a disease dependent on multi connections, enmeshed in the logics of a colonial counter science. In turn, one can argue that the hybrid form of social science fiction may be the most adequate way to think about the delirious products and unlikely networks of these colonial laboratories. Malaria as a disease figures largely there, an emblem of the simultaneously faithfully and fickle nature of postcolonial connectivity. Laboratories are sites of hard work and discovery, where theories and techniques are tested and new beings are created. Etymologically, "laboratory" is linked to labor and hardship, but also to labi, to slip, fall, or totter. Alien forms of animal, vegetable, and mineral circulate through them, and just as twentieth century labs created transuranic elements and transgenetic animals, colonial and postcolonial encounters produce transcultural and transhistorical entities, including xenotransfer between the species of social science and science fiction. Ghosh, however, describes a near future and not so distant past in which humans are reconfigured through technologies ranging from railroads to genetic reprogramming, reminding, as an anthropologist who has worked in Guatemala for eighteen years, that mechanical and biological experiments are nothing new for colonized peoples, their sinews, hearts, minds, bodies, and germlines repeatedly have been used in the service of alien invaders. In Ghosh's books, however, and in the "real world" the colonizers themselves are visited and sometimes reprogrammed by encounters with other systems and by microscopic invaders like the malaria parasite, which has led to the development of the counterinsurgent field of Tropical Medicine, producing many Nobel Prize winners. Fever and dysentery are the 'generals' that defend hot countries against our incursions and prevent us from replacing the aborigines that we have to make use off," complained a French colonial official in 1908.. The milieu of colonial laboratories produces strange alliances and emergent forms of the human.

Ghosh is concerned with the tropies, as the hot, fertile, colonial spaces in which the "human" is hypothesized, tested, and re mapped and in the sense of the tropes or figures that serve as lab equipment. Storytelling it self, the process of finding things out, is a central actant in *The Calcutta Chromosome.* Similarly one can suggest that social science fiction may itself be a tropical laboratory where one might dissect and examine the labour of other colonial labs and produce new ways of figuring the human. What might be called the postcolonial human has been defined through stories, like the debates over mass murder and enslavement that asked whether the naked creatures "discovered" in the brave new world even counted as human. In our existing world, however, all we cyborgs tend to the complex concatenations of both kinds of interventions, and *The Calcutta Chromosome* explores a range of human technology interfaces, from railroads, computers, and bureaucracies to genetic engineering and the mysterious workings of the malaria plasmodia.

The novel gives us technologies to work on the new human emerging from the tropics via tropes and troops, through analysis of mechanist and shaper transformations from alchemical networkings and interventions in the germline to immune system defenses and forms of reproduction that circumvent the Darwinian bottleneck of heterosexuality, Ghosh's *The Calcutta Chromosome* is a tropical laboratory about various forms of colonial laboratories. Two of its main characters, Antar and Murugan appeared in epigraph,. and they assist dissection and recombination of fiction, science, the social science fiction and social science. If one sets aside the publicity and marketing rhetoric that frames *The Calcutta Chromosome,* the science fiction label that has ascribed to the novel becomes more complicated. According to Samvel Delany's definition of the genre, Ghosh's novel is easily classified as science fiction since it "eals with what could have happened: that which is neither impossible nor verifiably possible. The only rule governing our response to science fiction – is that actions must be in accord with what we know of the physically explainable universe." Ava's capabilities would certainly fall into that rather region between possible and impossible. At the same time, however, the conspiracy theory that the novel posits concerning malaria research falls into that same neither region; it too seems neither possible nor verifiably impossible, and yet it mostly takes place in a distinctly un-science fiction like setting; 19* century India. In his 1979 study of science fiction novels, Gary Wolfe adds to Delany's general definition by identify a number of more specific elements that set science fiction as a distinct genre. According to Wolfe, most science fiction is ultimately concerned with transforming the unknown into the known. Of course, the known or unknown binary can be found in many other types of fiction, detective fiction and thrillers being the most obvious examples. What set science fiction apart for Wolfe is the distinct iconography that the genre uses to explore the known or unknown theme? From H. G. Wells through to Isaac Asimov, Wolfe identifies five icons that science fiction writers repeatedly make use of in their writing: The spaceship, the city, the wasteland, the robot and the monster. Depending on the writer, some stories may make use of only one of these icons, while others may rely on them all.

The novel is in many ways clearly interested in the struggle to make the unknown known, it relies on few if any of the icons Wolfe believe necessary to science fiction texts, of the five, the city is only icon that might be present, of the two cities in *The Calcutta Chromosome* Kolkatta and New York, the latter is the only one of real interest in terms of science fiction iconography since the scenes set in Kolkatta take place either in the distant past or recent past or almost present, But even the 21st century New York Ghosh portrays barely fits with the traditional science fiction city. According to Wolfe, cities in science fiction have a number of distinctive characteristics, few of which *The Calcutta* Chromosome New York possess. The city, for instance, is generally a confined space from which one must escape the "conformity of the densely urban environment" a conformity that is enforced by "a governmental system in which the police play an increasingly important role." While Antar dreams of leaving New York and retiring to Egypt, it is not New York city that prevents him from leaving so much as it is his commitment to the international water council and his dependence on their pension. Furthermore, although there are some authoritarian forces present, Antar's pay is docked for his doing personal reading while working, for example, none of this authority is imposed by the government nor by its police agent on behalf of the city or country.

Nor is the city a xenophobic one that "Promotes a distrust of what might lie outside of the projective boundaries of the collective society". Ghosh's conception of the 21st century resembles a McLuh-anesque "global village" much more than it does a series of closed and protected city-states. *The Calcutta Chromosome's* New York appears to have no protective boundary of any kind, its population being seemingly much more international and heterogeneous then native born and homogeneous. The regulars at the Penn station coffee shop include a Sudanese bank-teller, a Guyanese woman and Bangladeshi man, while the apartment building Antar lives in has attracted, "Middle Eastern and Central Asian families - Kurds, Afghans, Tajiks and Even a few Egyptians". Ultimately, regardless of the traits it may or may not share with the conventional science fiction city, *The Calcutta Chromosome's* 21st century New York has such a limited presence and direct relevance to the overall narrative that its importance as an icon is severely compromised.

Other aspects of the novel outside of Wolfe's icons give the book its science fiction qualities. Ava's presence, for instance, has some science fiction connotations: She is certainly more advanced than most computers available to people working out of their homes today. In fifteen minutes, for instance, she is able to trace a lost email by "Sifting through about six thousand eight hundred and ninety two trillion cunabytes - roughly eighty five billion times the estimated sum of every dactlyographic act every performed by a human being," and reconstruct it "by running the retrieved fragment through a storyline algorithm"" But in the end, even Ava is a weak defense of *The Calcutta Chromosome* science fiction identity since, despite her importance in helping Antar unite the disparate fragments of the story, the fact remains that the majority of the story occurs without Ava and her technological advancements; it is Murugan the science historian, using rather conventional techniques like archival research, who pieces the story together.

Ultimately, few of the obvious science fiction signifiers are really necessary to the overall structure and plot of the novel. The city and the futuristic setting provide an interesting context for the story but are largely unnecessary to the novel's final outcome. Really, the only necessary science fiction device central to the plot is the all knowing, all-powerful computer; it is Ava who in the end pieces the information together for Antar and the reader. Despite her importance, however, many of the crucial events in the story occur in a time and place for removed from Ava's presence.

With such tenuous links to science fiction, it might be useful, as Ball and Aull suggest, to instead consider *The Calcutta Chromosome* within a post colonial frame work. In their 1989 overview of post colonial writing, *The Empire Writes Back,* Bill Ashcroft, Gareth Griffiths and Helen Tiffin identify a number of recurring themes and icons that characterize postcolonial literatures, a number of which are also found in *The Calcutta Chromosome.* The use of a house as metaphor is a good example of a recurring postcolonial trope found in *The Calcutta Chromosome.* In the novel there are three house or buildings that might be read as metonymic structures in the text. The first is Antar's decaying building in New York, symbolic in many ways of Antar's migrant existence in 21st century United States. When Antar first arrived in New York with his wife, the building was full of apartments teeming with families and was full of life.

> "There was a time when there were nothing but apartments in the building, all rented to families; large, noisy, Middle Eastern and Central Asian families .... Kurds, Afghans, Tajiks and even a few Egyptians". [13]

By the time the reader meets Antar, however, most of the apartments, and the families that once lived in them, have been replaced by "warehouses and storage spaces", and the building is now more closely associated with sickness and death than with life. When Antar thinks back on the people who once lived in the building, those who most readily come to mind are those who were some how diseased or who suffered untimely deaths. His wife and unborn child are killed.

> "In the end it didn't matter: an amniotic embolism killed her and the baby in the thirty fifth week of her pregnancy". [13]

The chess player next door began to "Waste way" one summer while the woman in the apartment below is murdered by the delivery boy who battered "her head in with a cast iron skillet. The stagnant and sick atmosphere of the building reflects Antar's own stagnant and diseased existence. Antar, like his home, has been left behind and forsaken by the modern age. The second house of some symbolic importance in the novel is the colonial "bungalow" Ronald Ross lives in while working in Secunderabad. Through Murugan the house is set up as an obvious symbol of colonial decadence.:

> "He calls it a bungalow, but don't let him fool you: This place has a couple of dozen rooms, and half an acre of garden. Then there are the servants' quarters, way outback, where you can hardly see them: a long, low line of rooms. The rooms are pretty small, but some of them have Six or Seven people living inside and some have whole families in residence". [75]

The size and set up of the house is of little importance to the events in the novel. By dwelling on this otherwise insignificant detail, however, Murugan hints that the colonial inequalities that may seem to be a secondary importance may in fact be central to understanding the course of events in the novel. The houses and buildings of particular importance in postcolonial fiction, however, are those being demolished or under construction, an image that Ghosh places right at the centre of the novel.

> "At the far and of the room was a small balcony. Crossing the room, Murugan went out, leaned over the balustrade and looked up and down the street-from the tree lined cemetery at the London street and, to the traffic on London street, to his right".

"Shading his eyes, he threw a glance diagonally across at number three Robinson Street". [70]

Romen Haldar is renovating and allowing his group of counter scientists to use as a meeting place is the same house Ronald Ross lived in while working in Kolkatta at the turn of the century. In this case, it is difficult not to read some postcolonial significance into the fact that Indians and Nepalis have dismantled the house's interior and the "the entire construction gang was living in the gutted shell of the house. At the centre of the novel, then is the deconstruction of a colonial structure by former colonized subjects who are using the building to celebrate their distinctly Indian and non-colonial achievements in area of malaria research. There is more than just the central image of the house, however, to lend credence to the notion that the novel is at least partially postcolonial in nature. The alternative history that the novel proposes and its reworking of the 'official' metanarrative is also a common theme is post colonial literature. By reinterpreting historical fragments the novel is able to undermine the authority of colonial narratives. Not only does the novel present the official history of malaria research as an elaborate facade, but even more radically, it also suggests that this facade W.O.S. constructed by the colonized who used the colonizers as unwitting pawns in their scheme. Furthermore, in deconstructing one history and constructing another, Ghosh, like a number of other postcolonial writers, disrupts the conventional binary between the centre and the margin.

The Calcutta Chromosome destabilizes the 'Center' by focusing on the actions of otherwise peripheral characters. Murugan, for instance, the character at the center of the novel, is marginalized in numerous ways by society, both eccentric. The scientific community "brands Murugan as a crank and an eccentric" because of his outrageous theories, and the History of science society subsequently takes "the unprecedented step of revoking his membership." His colleagues at Life watch to be "erratic and obsessional" characterize his behaviour. Moreover, throughout the novel his "Psychological normalcy" is also called into question; Murugan himself hints that his bouts of syphilis and malaria might have somehow affected his brain, and by the end, of course, Antar finds him in an asylum. And yet despite Murugan's marginality, most of the information and events central to the story's development are filtered through him. Like Murugan, the group of counter scientists who are both at the centre of the novel and at the centre of malaria research 'and discovery operate and exert their control from the margins of society and scientific discourse. The colonial scientists as deviating from the psychological norms characterize the woman in charge, Mangala –

> "Farley felt the blood rushing to his face. Don't pay her any attention, Cunningham said to Parley, with a wink, she's a little touched – you know". [119]

Likewise, the work she is overseeing is often set up in binary opposition to the accepted centre. For Murugan, just as there are "matter and antimatter," "rooms and anterooms and Christ and Antichrist," there are "Science and counter science" practiced by "fring people, marginal types so far from the mainstream you can't see them from the shore." The discoveries of the counter scientists always occur outside of the scientific centre, subversive alternatives to the 'accepted' European scientific experiments. Murugan even uses the "other mind" theory to describe their work, a label fraught with postcolonial connotations. That it is Murugan, a marginal character in his own right, who position these people as peripheral says a great deal about just how far removed from the centre they ar~.

Of particulars significance to the relationship Ghosh establishes between the margin and center in the novel is Parley's visit to Cunningham's lab to test Laveran's theories. While in the lab. Farley becomes a first hand witness to the counter-scientists' literal displacement of the center and the shifting of power towards the margins. During his first day in the lab Parley sees, through a reflection in his glass of water, that it is Mangala, the one, according to Cunningham, who is "not all there" who is choosing the slides and in effect running the lab. Determined to find out what Mangala and Lutchman are doing, he decides to return the following day. Upon arriving the next day, Parley notices "a great deal of activity in a nearby anteroom". Just as one day before he sees nothing of importance in Cunningham's slides, slides that are results of experiments made in what "Was once one of the best equipped research laboratories in the whole Indian subcontinent." Parley soon realizes that everything of importance going on in the lab is occurring in the anteroom and not in the laboratory proper. After threatening to say all night he watches Lutchman snatch "up a set of clean slides," then slip "away to the anteroom."

> "Once, he was gone, Parley made his way silently across the laboratory. Flattening himself against the wall, he crept towards the door until he had maneuvered himself into a position where he could look into the anteroom without himself being detected. Parley had steeled himself for anything, or so he thought, but he was unprepared for what he saw next". [127]

Here, with the separation between room and anteroom, the figurative binary opposition between margin and centre becomes literal. This peripheral room and the counter science occurring therein become of central importance and in turn displace the colonial lab and its conventional approaches to science from its position of authority. In the end, the most interesting aspect of Ghosh's novel is not the degree to which it is either a science fiction novel or a postcolonial text but the ways in which Ghosh brings the two very different conventions together to create something new, a hybrid novel that draws attention to different themes by casting them in a new light. Its hybridity can be explored through a number of examples, but it is in the novel's use of silence that is the key to understanding its hybridity. Through silence,

Ghosh pits conventions of science fiction and post colonialism against one another and succeeds in problematizing the notions of borders and barriers and the known or unknown binary in both literary traditions. Silence in *The Calcutta Chromosome* is both a science fiction barrier that must be overcome in order to expose the unknown and a postcolonial means of resisting the dominant discourse and defending knowledge against unwanted appropriation.

All of the recurring icons Wolfe finds in science fiction he traces to the "image of the barrier". Certainly barriers are not unique to science fiction; postcolonial texts, including Ghosh's previous novels, are replete with barriers of different kinds. In an interview with Ghosh, Eleanor Wachtel comments "Borders, boundaries - whether real or imagined, natural or artificial, whether political or social, the boundaries and borders that divide people and places figure very prominently in your work". But it is not any kind of barrier or boundary that Wolfe sees recurring in science fiction, but specifically those barriers that separate "the known from the unknown beyond the barrier is the unknown, or Chaos, and in this Chaos is the knowledge that will enable the Society to sustain its impetus of growth." Thus, although *The Calcutta Chromosome* does not rely on any of the specific icons normally employed by science fiction writers to symbolize the barrier, it still has at its core the central image of a barrier. According to Murugan;

> "Now, let's say there was something like science and counter science? Thinking of it the abstract, wouldn't you say that the first Principal of a functioning counter science would have to be secrecy? – It would have to use secrecy as a technique or procedure. It would in principle have to refuse all direct communication, straight off the bat, because to communicate, to put ideas into language would be to establish a claim to know which is the first thing that a counter science would dispute". [88]

The counter scientists silence and secrecy create a barrier that Murugan and by extension Antar spend the entire novel trying to break through. Murugan especially is interested in the unspoken "new knowledge" that the counter scientists are projecting behind their silence as well as being an example of a barrier in the science fiction tradition silence of course is also a common trope of resistance in other literatures Feminist critics, for instance have demonstrated its importance in texts by women. In postcolonial text it may take any number of different forms depending on the writer and the particular tradition out of which they are writing.

Understand this way, silence is something imposed by the state to control it's subjects; it somehow must be over come if the oppressed hope to gain any knowledge or power silence however when practiced by the oppressed or subjected, can sometime the power structure or even be a source of power in it's own right.

It is of course, an unequal exchange of knowledge. The knowledge being imparted by the teacher will ultimately be knowledge that support the teacher's position of power, the knowledge that the pupils offer on the other hand, will inevitably be used to further subjugate them and inscribe them within the existing power structure, the knowledge that a subject offers up to the authorities is no different, their knowledge is recorded and stored by creation of categories and system of names insane criminal and sinner and used to classify them and define their mode of being ultimately this archives of knowledge comes to constitute and uphold a regime of power. The novel is teeming with people and organizations engaged in Foucauldian endeavour to collect and classify as much information as possible. The international water commission through Ava and Antar are in the process of creating a vast archive of information in the hopes that They will be able to use it to their advantage in the future.

> "They saw Themselves making History with their vast water control experiment: They wanted to record every minute detail of what they had done, what They would do. Instead of having an historian sift through their dirt looking for meaning they wanted to do it themselves: they wanted to load their dirt with their own meanings". [86]

Murugan, for his part is involved in a similar process in documenting the development of Ronald Ross's malaria research of course the only reason Murugan has able to catalogue Ross life is that Ross himself wrote everything down There is also J. W. D. Grigson who like Murugan and Ross in the habit of collecting and recording visit amounts of information.

> "And where he goes Grigson takes notes. Boy does he take notes: he keeps a diary he keeps a journal when Ypsilanti collage brought his collected papers in 1999 They had to hire an eight axle truck to ship the stuff out There's nothing he does' not make a note of and that means nothing". [76]

In this atmosphere of near obsessive knowledge collecting and classifying, silence becomes one of the only effective means of resistance, to speak in this atmosphere is to be inscribed into the dominant discourse. In the novel, the contrast between Murugan's experiences and those of the counter scientists illustrates very clearly the potential effectiveness of using silence as a way of resisting inscription. The scientific establishment's 'rules' constantly however around Murugan and the counter-scientists, and around their respective endeavours. Murugan spends much to the novel offering up his knowledge to various examiners including Antar and Urmila. In his attempts to have people understand his theories he willingly offers up his knowledge to the scientific community, which in turn leads to his inscription by the dominant discourse. Both the summary of his research in an article entitled "Certain systematic Discrepancies in Ronald Ross's account of Plasmodium B". Positioned as a deviant from accepted norms, Murugan is no longer a treat; relegated to the margins, he is no longer taken seriously. There is little outcry, for instance, when the History of science society revokes his membership. The establishment is able to push him from the centre. Despite the fact that in the context of the novel his theories seem to be correct, voicing his opinions and providing evidence leaves him almost completely powerless by the end of the novel. The counter scientists, on the other hand, take the opposite approach in dealing with the scientific community. By working in secrete and remaining silent they are able to pursue their research without the powerlessness that normally comes from being marginal or eccentric. As Murugan sees it:

> "Fact is we're dealing with a crowd for whom silence is a religion. We don't even know what we don't know. We don't know who's in this and who's not; we do not know how much of the spin they're got under control. We don't know how many of the threads they want us to pull together and how many they want to keep hanging for whoever comes next". [180]

Because the counter scientists rarely impart any of their knowledge to any one, the dominant scientific discourse has nothing to use against them and cannot control or inscribe them the way they do Murugan. Like Murugan, these counter-scientists remain on the margins of the scientific establishment; unlike him, however, their marginalization is by choice and thus does not leave them powerless. It allows them the freedom and power to take the scientific inquiry off in directions unfathomable by conventional scientists. In fact, the counter scientists are in such control of knowledge exchange process that they have almost managed to reverse the power structure. In the example from Foucault quoted above, the examiner imparts some knowledge to his pupils in order to draw out different, potentially incriminating knowledge from them. In the novel the supposedly marginal counter scientists manage to put themselves in the position of authority by systematically releasing bits of knowledge in order to have the conventionally trained scientists unknowingly offer up more in return.

The Calcutta Chromosome is a serious novel written in the manner of a thriller. It is set in the near future but reaches back into the Victorian World. The protagonist, Antar is a cyber researcher who works at terminal in his apartment in a marginal New York neighborhood. From this unremarkable station, he helps to sort through a virtual rubbish leap of international bureaucracy, including not only documents but also all sorts of other detritus of "official" life, which is incessantly inventoried by a

Supercomputer called Ava. By chance, or so at first it seems, Antar comes across the identity card of Murugan, a former Co-worker who had disappeared in Calcutta while seeking to substantiate the theory that had consumed him and had made him a target of ridicule in the scientific community. Murugan had become convinced that Sir Ronald Ross's discovery of the mechanism by which mosquitoes transmit malaria was in fact the singular evidence of a conspiracy of "Counter Scientists" who had transcended western science in their recognition of its obverse. And so the seemingly simple accident in Antar's coming across one of Murugan's old identity cards provokes his dogged investigation of the incredibly convoluted complexities of Murugan's theory and of his disappearance.

In Ghosh's fictive world, a simple cause can have extraordinarily complex effects and a simple fact can contain the essence of extraordinarily complex truth, the pattern that under lies all of the diverse historical periods, geographical settings, characters, situations, and themes of this dense but gripping novel is analogous to the principal of phrase structure rules in generative grammar, that is an infinite number of variation can be generated from a very finite set of variables. This principle is, of course, evident in the very simple binary coding that has remained the basis of computer programming despite incredibly rapid advancements in hardware, operating systems, specialized software, networking, and multimedia applications. Likewise, this principle is evident in the mutability of the proto zoic parasite that the mosquito transfers into the bloodstream of the malaria sufferer. Though cellularly it is no more complex than the amoeba, this protozoan has the ability not only to enter into the blood cell that it then consumes but also to adopt the genetic characteristics of that cell making it extremely difficult to eradicate the parasite without further compromising its host. In the fictional science of Ghosh's novel, this mutuability can be traced to the so-called Calcutta chromosome.

Thus, the ancient metaphysics of reincarnation and the futuristic possibilities of genetic engineering become fictionally linked in a secret Indian cult that has discovered how to use the Calcutta chromosome to transfer their genetic essence through a succession of host bodies. Ultimately, Antar's connection to Ava, the supercomputer, becomes itself a mechanism for this sort of transference of identity. This eventuality pushes us well past cybernetics into a reality in which encoded data is served by, rather than serves, cellular biology. In *The Calcutta Chromosome,* Ghosh provides a multi-leveled exploration of issues of identity. As in his other books, Ghosh is concerned here with the contrasts between western and Eastern mindsets, with the cultural ramifications of the Diaspora of nonwestern peoples, and with the economic and political vulnerability of women, minorities populations, and other marginalized peoples.

But, more than anything else, Ghosh is concerned here with what defines identity at its most basic level. If we can imagine an entire individual being replicated or regenerated from a single sample of DNA, how are we now to define that the "Soul" or the "Self" ? This is truly an information age, how do we define ourselves if not as information, if not as data? That is, how can we continue to separate ourselves from the world outside of ourselves? If we can imagine a thought being transmitted or accessed like any other electronic transmission, how are we to separate the private and public aspects of our selves? Is the concept of "Privacy" to become as outdated as, say, the belief in guardian angel? If data can be copied to us much as viruses enter our bloodstreams, how are we to know exactly who or what we are? And, finally, if we can achieve immortality but only at the expense of our familiar physical selves, how can we measure our looses against our rejection of death?

The malarial protozoan is self-replicating. When it has exhausted its food source, when it has devoured a blood cell from the inside out, it dies and its offspring flood out into the bloodstream. Most of them also die in a brief, frantic search for new hosts, but a few do manage to insert themselves into other blood cells. Of course, when an individual dies of malaria, all of those protozoa perish with their host. The only survivors are those that have been carried to new hosts by mosquitoes. Thus, the models that this cycle provides is that of an arbitrary process by which expendable individuals insure the proliferation of the species.

Ghosh offers a mild dystopia here. Antar's New York is a more desolate, decrepit, and impersonal one than the present-day city, but Antar can still find convivial souls and his life isn't all too bad. Ghosh doesnot expend much energy on working out a vision of the future and didn't put too much thought into it. Antar's computer, known as Ava, is a pretty neat thing, able to speak in any dialect and do a good number of things, but otherwise Ghosh's future sounds out of date even these few years after he wrote it. His Internet is still expensive and slow, for example. And Antar's friends discuss "some new seam for saving on subway token," when it must have been clear even in 1995. That the subway token would soon be phased out, replaced by a more flexible electronic card system. Ghosh's quaint lack of imagination about the future is only appropriate because the focus of the book is on the past. The past first drops into Antar's lap, or rather; appears on his computer screen, in the form of a Piece of an ID card from another Life watch employee, Murugan. Murugan went missing in 1995 in Calcutta and, as it happens, Antar met him before then.

Murugan was obsessed with Ronald Ross, who had received the Nobel Prize for his work on malaria. With that the three timelines are set, and the novel shifts back and forth between them; there is Antar's present, as he investigates the ID card and what might have happened. There are the events leading up to Murugan's disappearance in 1995, which include his discussions with Antar and then his adventures in Kolkatta. At there are the events from the late 19th Century, as the malaria, discoveries are being made. It is complicated, and it gets more so. There are differ‹nt casts of characters, few in New York, more in Kolkattà, and a whole slewin in 19th Century India. Ross malaria related discoveries are the key. It turns out the discoveries are surprising, as is how he came to make them. And Murugan thinks there is more to them too, *The Calcutta Chromosome,* for one. The 'Steps of Ross' discovery where also remarkably fortuitous; they almost seem to fall into place for him and this is where Murugan focuses his attention. Murgan wants to follow Ross trail, and that of some of the mysterious figures around him. The malarial theories and what Ghosh does with them aren't bad. Ghosh has some clever ideas, and the stories meander along quite entertainingly for the most part. There are other figures in Kolkatta, a Journalist, a writer, and others, who play larger roles, and some of the story comes together quite nicely, unfortunately, however, Ghosh eventually settles for hokey mysticism rather than anything more soundly scientific, and the book tapers off to its predictable but unsatisfying conflation.

A major plot twist in *The Calcutta Chromosome* depends on the strange capacity of malaria to live dormant in a human body for years, even decades, and then suddenly blossom again into desperate chills and fevers up to 106 degrees. As Antar is decoding Murugan's whereabouts, he begins to feel a fever coming on, allying him, not completely willfully and quite unpredictably, to a counter technoscience. Malaria is less a disease than an interaction of processes, actors, and actants. A parasite, not mal aires or bad air from which it gets name, entering the bloodstream from a masquito bite and then migrating to the liver to replicate causes it and hide from the immune system for the same reason, it also tends to congregate in the placenta. It forms a cyst that bursts, sending parasites into the red blood cells sticky, foming a plaque that clogs the vascular system, including the capillaries of the brain. Malaria can kill by causing anemia, brain swelling, or organ failure from the fever. Those who survive the illness experience a much commented upon listlessness and malaise. The parasites go through a number of developmental stages, making a medical "magic bullet" hard to develop. They also develop immunity to the favored cures, quinine and its chemical replicants.

Malaria is a vector-transmitted disease. Female mosquitoes ingest blood to fuel the production of eggs. Those that bite humans generally do so at night. Then, heavily laden, they sit on the nearest vertical surface to digest the meal. Later, the mosquito will lay her eggs in nearby standing water, where they develop into larvae and then more mosquitoes. Sick people become a parasite reservoir the mosquitoes dip into and can be back into the world. With the vector's help, a single human carrier can infect over one hundred others. Mosquitoes in their various forms eggs, larvae, adults, seem to travel easily in ships and airplanes, as do the parasites carried inside human bodies moving around the globe. It's all about what's in between, between human, vector, and parasite, and how these connect humans across space and, in Ghosh's novel, time as a newspaper headline recently put it. In Ghosh's novel, the Calcutta chromosome lashes together rich and poor, in India and in Diaspora, it links Egyptian and Journalist and Hollywood star, a self made man and nineteenth century laboratory assistant, colonial science and post colonial counter science and a social scientist.

In the end, the novel is perhaps more post colonial than the publicity surrounding it gives it credit for. *The Calcutta Chromosome's* greatest strength lies in its success at blending the post colonial with science fiction tradition. Placed as they are in the science fiction framework Ghosh sets up, the familiar post colonial tropes of borders and resistance become unfamiliar and begs a closer examination. Ultimately, the novel forces readers to abandon their pre conceived notions regarding our often-arbitrary classifications of literature. There is no reason a past colonial novel cannot employ science fiction tropes or vice versa. Success, as we can see in *The Calcutta Chromosome,* lies in being able to successfully exploit a given genre's or tradition's strength and themes to best suit one's ultimate objectives. In his interrogation of the discourses of science and technology Ghosh primarily explores how Europeans and Indians exchanged sacred and scientific ideas.

The main narrative of the novel involves a re-examination of the history of late nineteenth-century malaria research by a possibly deranged Calcutta-born man named Murugan [he is also known as Morgan] who works for an international public health company called Life Watch and uses an Americanized slang register, which character-izes him as a Diaspora subject. Murugan has had a life-long obsession with the history of malaria research, which has led him to the con-viction that Ronald Ross, the British scientist who was awarded the 1902 Nobel Prize for Medicine for his work on the life-cycle of the malaria parasite which four years earlier had isolated how the disease is transmitted, was not a 'lone genius' [57], a brilliant British dilettante who outstripped all of the contemporary scientists in the field. Murugan believes there is a secret history that has been erased from the scribal records of the colonial society and from medical historiography more generally. He has devoted himself to uncovering the hidden truth.

Murugan is first encountered through the mediation of another Diaspora subject, Antar, a New York-based computer systems opera-tor, who has been a former colleague of Murugan's and now works for an international water agency, which has absorbed Life Watch. In the opening chapter Antar comes across a fragment of an ID card on the screen of his computer and this sets him off on a quest to reconstruct the totality of the card and then the recent life-history of its missing owner. The owner turns out to be Murugan, a man whom Antar has interviewed a few years before -the novel is set in the near future - on behalf of Life Watch, to try to dissuade him from a request to be transferred to Calcutta, at a greatly reduced salary, so that he can pursue his 'notion of the so-called 'Other Mind': a theory that some person or persons had systematically interfered with Ronald Ross's experiments to push malaria research in certain directions while lead-ing it away from others' [36] Murugan has been reported as missing; he has last been seen in Calcutta on 21 August 1995.

From this departure-point the novel uncovers its intricate network of traces, interweaving a number of parallel quest-stories which range from those of Ross and his late nineteenth-century medical contem-poraries through to An tar's pursuit of Murugan through the resources of the Internet, which at this moment in the near future has already become considerably more sophisticated than it was at the time when the novel was published.

In *The Calcutta Chromosome* the Web as-sumes much the same role as weaving in Ghosh's earlier work, functioning as a synecdoche for the interpenetration of cultures, which as I have indicated is central to all of Ghosh's writing. Antar's quest for Murugan leads the reader into a Russian doll-like assortment of other quests, which are gradually revealed to be interlocking narrat-ives and which, to borrow Dixon's phrase, again inhabit 'a discursive space that flows across political and national boundaries, and even across generations in time'. In this sense at least, *The Calcutta Chromo-some,* which initially seems to be very different from *The Shadow Lines,* is exploring very similar terrain.

A single example of the novel's numerous interlocking narrative strands may help to illustrate how its linkages across time and space operate. On the day on which Murugan arrives in Calcutta, 20 August 1995, Phulboni, a famous writer, is being given an award to mark his eighty-fifth birthday. Receiving the award, Phulboni gives a gnomic speech about the power of silence. Like Murugan / Morgan, Phulboni has more than one name, more than one identity. His 'real name' [27] is Saiyad Murad Husain; Phulboni is a pen-name. In his earlier life Phulboni has undergone a mysterious experience, when, as a young recruit to a British company, he was sent, in 1933, to a provincial town named Renupur. He has arrived by train at its deserted station, some distance from the town and in a landscape flooded by monsoon rains; and there, despite the stationmaster's attempts to persuade him to the contrary, he decides to spend the night in the signal-room. A night of terror ensues. Objects move as though controlled by some telekinetic agency. Phulboni falls asleep, awakes to discover that the signal lantern is no longer where he has placed it and then sees it some fifty yards down the railway track. Assuming that the stationmaster is carrying it, he follows it down the line, trips and narrowly averts being killed by a train, which comes hurtling down the track at this moment, even though the line is a siding and no train is due. In fact the stationmaster has told him that the station has only ever been used once before. He appears to fall asleep again and wake up the next morning to find the stationmaster telling him that the lantern has not been moved. And then he appears to awaken again, just in time to throw himself out of the path of *another* oncoming train. This time the experience is 'all too real' [279]. Phulboni subsequently speaks to the train's stokers and engineers, who are horrified that it has been directed into the siding, which they say has not been used for thirty years and where the tracks are rusty, overgrown and full of debris. When Phulboni suggests that the stationmaster may have 'pulled the switch by mistake' [279], the chief engineer of the train tells him there has not been a stationmaster at Renupur for thirty years.

The first part of this episode could well be explained away as Phulboni's fantasy or hallucination and the text is full of incidents which raise the possibility that those who experience them are Pynchonesque paranoid schizophrenics or fever-prone former malaria sufferers, experiencing recurrent bouts of delirium – Antar, Murugan and Ross have all contracted malaria at some point in their lives - but, as in Pynchon [1966: 13], there is a body of circumstantial evidence to suggest that the dangers faced by the text's questers are 'all too real' and that a secret Manichean counter-force may be at large in the world. Rather more than thirty years previously, in 1894, an American scientist, Elijah Parley, who appears to have discovered that a sinister conspiracy is manipulating the experiments of Ross's Calcutta predecessor, D.D. Cunningham (also known as C.C. Dunn), has been reported as having vanished after disembarking from a train at Renupur. Like virtually everything else in the text the nature of this report is presented as unreliable: it takes the form of An tar's super-computer Ava's partly fictionalized reconstruction of a lost e-mail account of Parley's missing last letter, a letter which has itself mysteriously disappeared after Murugan has read it in a Baltimore library. Nevertheless it posits the possibility of a startling link with the Phulboni episode. In this episode the veteran guard of the train that has nearly killed Phulboni remem-bers a foreigner dying at Renupur in 1894 in an almost identical inci-dent. At the time of the foreigner's death the sole occupant of the station was a young man named Laakhan. Laakhan [also know as Lutchman - the shifting nature of names is a clue to the text's central revelation concerning the Calcutta chromosome which still lies ahead] has been one of the assistants in Cunningham's laboratory, whose conspiratorial activities Parley appears to have discovered. Hence, at least according to one interpretation, the need to eliminate Parley. And by this point in the novel, which employs a Conradian battery of time-shifts, the reader knows that Laakhan / Lutchman has subsequently worked for Ross and there are also traces of his identity in a range of other contexts. He has a thumbless left hand and in the Phulboni episode, along with the evidence of poltergeist activity Phulboni has seen a mysterious imprint of just such a hand in the signal-box at Renupur. The elderly guard completes the story of what happened at Renupur in 1894 by telling Phulboni that, after the death of the foreigner, a stationmaster *was* found, an upper-caste man who re-garded Laakhan and his misshapen left hand as worse than untouch-able and attempted to kill him 'by switching the points and leading him before a train' [281], only to suffer the fate he has intended for Laakhan himself - a third instance of a narrowly averted or actual death of this kind.

In some ways this third instance is the most interesting, though it is narrated in a more summary fashion, since it provides the most obvious case of a subaltern figure exercising power, even if this figure remains voiceless, an antagonist rather than a protagonist in the text's storytelling process. There will be a fourth trace of the Renupur station motif towards the end of the novel.

What Farley has discovered is that Cunningham's work on the mos-quito parasite is being hampered by assistants he has picked up at Sealdah railway station in Calcutta: notably Laakhan and a woman, who in the text's imaginative reconstruction of these events is named Mangala. She appears to be both the high priestess of a secret medical cult offering a cure for syphilis and the brain behind the discoveries that will eventually lead to Ross's winning the Nobel Prize. So Ghosh's narrative discredits the Western scientist and instates an Indian female subaltern in his place.

Murugan's research leads him to the conclusion that Mangala and her associates are hindering Cunningham's research so that Ross, whom they can use as a vessel for their discoveries, will replace him. These discoveries are, however, concerned with far more than a mala-ria cure. They involve a counter-epistemology, which promises a form of immortality through the erosion of Western conceptions of discrete subjectivity, through the dismantling of the shadow-lines that con-struct notions of autonomous selfhood. This perhaps explains the text's recurrent destabilizing of notions of fixed identity by giving characters more than one name. Mangala's discovery of the means by which malaria is transmitted has come about as a by-product of her real research interest. Working outside the straitjacket of Western empiri-cal methodologies, she has been attempting to evolve 'a technology for interpersonal transference' [106], a means of transmitting knowledge 'chromosomally from body to body' [107]. In Murugan's view, the relationship between Mangala's counter-science and that of conven-tional scientists such as Ross is analogous to the relationship between 'matter and antimatter [. . .] rooms and ante-rooms [. . .] Christ and Antichrist and so on' (103). So, if one accepts Murugan's thesis, there is the possibility of a subaltern Manichean force that, though it operates through silence and secrecy, is at least as powerful as Western logocentrism. In this respect the novel is strongly reminiscent of Pynchon's *The Crying of Lot 49* (1966), where the protagonist finds traces of an alternative communications network, which appears to have been functioning in America - and prior to this in Renaissance Europe - as a hidden, but omnipresent Manichean system. Whether such a conspiracy exists or whether it is simply the product of a paranoiac's fantasizing is the central debate in *The Crying of Lot 49* and the novel concludes with this question left unanswered.

In one sense, *The Calcutta Chromosome* is equally open-ended.. Towards the end Antar receives information about Murugan's disap-pearance. He, too, has taken a train to Renupur and so it seems as though he may have suffered the fate of Parley and the stationmaster who has attempted to kill Laakhan. However, towards the end Ava, Antar's computer, locates him in the Department of Alternative States in Fort William, Calcutta; he has become a psychiatric patient. At this point Antar himself is feverish as a result of a recurrence of his malaria. So both the main interpreters of the evidence are, from one point of view, extremely unreliable. But, then, all of Ghosh's work suggests that the imaginative, fictive reconstruction of subaltern experience is the only way in which it can be rendered. Hence is his blurring of the bound-aries between anthropology and fiction. If one admits that fictive invention can operate in this way, then the reliability of the centers of consciousness that are experiencing the action ceases to be such a seri-ous issue.

This is not to suggest that Ghosh engages in a playful postmodernist relativism, however. What *The Calcutta Chromosome* forces its readers to engage with is the possibility of an alternative historiography, in which traditionally disempowered subjects prove to be the real pup-pet-masters. The counter-science cult led by Mangala can only operate through silence -Phulboni's disquisition on the power of silence on his eighty-fifth birthday is the single passage which [paradoxically?] articulates this - but the fictive reconstruction in which Murugan, Antar and ultimately Ghosh engage subverts the hegemonic domi-nance of Western logocentrism all the same. And this has implications for readings of colonial and post-colonial cultural practices that em-phasize Manichean allegory. According to Jan Mohamed such allegory is a Western discourse, which constructs binary oppositions in which the colonial subject is always the inferior partner in a two-way power relationship. But orthodox Augustinian theology, which is the lynch-pin of Western Christianity, regards Manicheism as a heresy because it propounds dualistic modes of classification. It is a heresy because it allows evil to exist in the world as a counter-force to good, whereas the orthodox position denies evil any such autonomous existence. Since God is omnipresent, evil can only be the privation of good. So post-colonial critics whose concern with the construction of alteration leads them to suggest that Western colonialism habitually operated in terms of Manichean classifications are in fact proposing a model which is at odds with the dominant view of Manicheism in European thought. Of course, Western attitudes may have changed in the late Victorian heyday of Empire, but the popular post-colonial version of

Manicheism still distorts because it obscures the fact that classic Western discourse has been monistic not dualistic. Manicheism is more accurately characterized as an Eastern challenge to the exclusiveness of Western discourses which deny the Other's capacity for utterance.

Ghosh engages with Manicheism in an altogether more complex and historically grounded way than the post-colonial interpreters of Manichean allegory. He only mentions it as such on one occasion in the novel [214]. This is in a passage about the archaeological excavations of a woman who has been a devotee of a 'Society of Spiritualists' that flourished in Madras at the same time as the Theosophical So-ciety, which with its Gnostic beliefs was itself a late nineteenth-century challenge to Western monism. However, the Society is led by a woman who is seen as Madame Blavatsky's 'arch-rival' [207] and her disciple, the Hungarian Countess Pongracz, whom Antar appears to have met during his early life in Egypt [5-7], has become an advocate of the teachings of Valentinus [the Alexandrian-born Gnostic philosopher who took dualistic religious beliefs to Rome in the second century AD], as well as an excavator of archaeological traces of dualistic systems - Nestorian as well as Manichean. Like the Countess Pongracz, Ghosh discovers fragments of suppressed heterodox systems; and the novel's repeated emphasis on Silence provides a reading of the subaltern which suggests that a figure denied a voice by hegemonic cultures and deemed heretical in Christian thinking could exist as a viable power-player in his and, in this case even more, her own right.

The Calcutta chromosome and the possibility of effecting the 'interpersonal transference' of knowledge occupies a central role in this investigation, since such transference would erode the barriers between elite and subaltern classes, between the purveyors and the recipients of knowledge. Everything about Ghosh's novel seems to be working towards this end. Structurally it moves between multiple stories and characters; and the near-repetition of variant forms of the same situation, such as the Renupur-station episode, also works to dismantle the notion of discrete essentialist versions.

In addition to all this, there is a final twist in the narrative, which takes the investigation of epistemological relationships into yet more subtle territory. Throughout the text readers are made aware that the borderline between discoverers and those who are discovered is an extremely porous one. Ross appears to be a discoverer who makes a revolutionary advance in the science of microscopy, but it seems he has been discovered and controlled by Mangala and her followers. Murugan investigates the secret history of malaria research and is in turn investigated by Antar. The last two chapters of the novel complicate and extend this pattern even further. On 21 August 1995 Murugan follows the final stages of his trail with a magazine journalist, Urmila Roy, another quester who has been prominent throughout the novel. His thesis involves the belief that the counter-science cult is absorbed with 'interpersonal transference' as part of a long-term strategy based on the notion that' to know something is to change it' [104]. Towards the end the novel appears to be moving towards some kind of apocalyptic revelation and one wonders whether Murugan is about to become a victim or an initiate of the cult. Such ambivalence is, of course, central to *The Calcutta Chromosomes* procedure and its unsettling of the shadow-lines between elite and subaltern subjects. Nevertheless there is a fresh surprise in the penultimate chapter when Murugan tells Urmila that *she is* the 'chosen' [306] one of Mangala's contemporary incarnations and asks her to promise, 'that you'll take me across if I don't make it on my own' [305]. Urmila's investigations have played a significant part in Murugan's detective-work, but hitherto she has not seemed to occupy a central role in the process of discovery. Now Murugan sees her as having such a role and explains:

> "You see, for them the only way to escape the tyranny of knowledge is to turn it on itself. But for that to work they have to create a single perfect moment of discovery when the person who discovers is also that which is discovered". [306]

As one closes *The Calcutta Chromosome,* there is perhaps yet one more inference to be drawn from the novel. In erasing the distinction between discoverers and the discovered, Ghosh has also demonstrated the unsatisfactoriness of making rigid distinctions between storytellers and listeners. Nobody, the suggestion seems to be, is exempt from history or from playing an active role in the *historiogmphical* process. So, perhaps the ultimate discoverer who is discovered by the novel is the reader. *The Calcutta Chromosome* has invited its readers to play the role of hermeneutic detective, to piece together its numerous clues to arrive, if not at a solution, at least at a possible version of meaning. The final insistence that all the investigators within the text are implicated in the material they are investigating leaves the novel's readers having to consider the possibility that they too are caught in the conspiracy of history. Or, to put it in another way, the conclusion suggests that readers have not been playing the role of passive subalterns, but rather, as makers of meaning, empowering themselves through the *silent* agency of reading. For adherents of reader response theory, such a dis-covery will come as nothing new, but the novel's contribution to such debates remains a highly distinctive one, because it provides a site which combines a re-reading of fashionable post-colonial theorizing about Manichean allegory with this dismantling of the Manichean binary of writer and reader.

WORKS CITED

Ghosh Amitav. *The Calcutta Chromosome,* New Delhi: Ravi Dayal Publisher, 2002.

Pynchon, Thomas. *The Crying of Lot 49*, Philadelphia : J. B. Lippincott, 1966.

Bourjaely, Vance, 'A certain kind of work In *Afterwards*' ed. Thomas McCormack, quoted in Higdon.

Jameson, Frederick. *Marxism and Form*, New Jersey, 1971.

Bhatt, Indira. 'Disappearances and Discovery a study of Amitav Ghosh's *The Calcutta Chromosome*' in *50 Years of Indian Writing*, ed. by R.K. Dhawan, IAES, New Delhi, 1999.

Mukherjee, Meenakshi, 'Review in India Today', May 15, 1996.

6

The Glass Palace

Amitav Ghosh's novel, *The Glass Palace* opens with a new and unintelligible sound. It is a sound that comes surging across the plain into Mandalay, Burma, traveling up the banks of the Irrawaddy River, Skidding across the western wall of the Mandalay Fort, and ultimately spreading confusion in the marketplace. With gentle irony, the narrator tells us that the only person who can identify the sound correctly, it is British cannon as the army advances on defiant Burma in the 1880, is Rajkumar, who is merely an Indian and only a boy and thus not to be believed. In this way, the opening of Ghosh's *The Glass Palace* beautifully ushers the reader into a world of sensations, crowds, symbols and boundaries the rest fragile and suspended in the face of global forces. As this impressive historical novel unfolds over 100 years and across the borders of Burma, India and Malaya, it reminds us how globalization is not a recent invention of late 20th Century capitalism, but rather a phenomenon with a long and complex history that insinuates itself into other histories, whether national, communal, familiar or, perhaps most threateningly personal.

The opening scene of *The Glass Palace* also introduces us to a question that is repeated throughout this momentous epic narrative, the question authority and, in particular, the authority to interpret new signs as they appear on the constantly changing landscape of colonized territory. Question of economic, artistic, cultural and national authority emerge in the novel's portrayal of two families over three generations, pushed apart and pulled together by the forces of capitalism, Colonialism and insurgency movement. It is Ghosh's particular talent to interlace these questions with the telling of his characters, live and to use them to probe deeply into the intricate nature of colonialism as it is lived on a daily level and as its legacy is transmitted over time.

Although the British formally left India more than half a century age, their presence still sits at the centre of that culture. It has been tempting, too tempting, perhaps, to place all the Indian writers recently so conspicuous in the west on a spectrum represented at its poles by Salman Rushdie on the left, trying to get back at the Empire by turning its very language and literature into sentences as crowded and noisy as the streets of an Indian city, and on the right, V S. Naipaul, perfecting a style more Augustan and austere than even that of his historical masters, and writing with a self conscious concern for clarity and for making fastidious discriminations, in an international world ever more without a centre. The distinction is a political one, of course, as well as a generational one, but on neither side have any Indian writers been able to find a resolution of their competing literary legacies as sonorous or affirmative as that, say, of Derek Walcott. Midnight's grandchildren look a little like children in the wake of a messy divorce, having to choose between an imperial father who's gone off to lick his wounds and an indigenous mother who, though supportive, seems a little lost.

As the American Empire makes its presence more urgently felt in India, and as the west itself begins to be colonized by young Indians in their thirties, the old divisions have at last begun to fade. Many of the most accomplished 'Indian writers' now in view refuse to be placed within the old colonial frame. Arundhati Roy, in her *God of Small Things,* addresses the age old Indian theme of caste in a style that seems driven by a Lawrentian fury and a cinematic sense of structure, with very little of classic English literature behind it; Abraham Verghese, born to Indian parents in Ethiopia, trains his compassionate diasporan eye on the shifting migrant cultures that overlap in the American South; and Pankaj Mishra, in his impressively lucid and inartificial first novel, *The Romantics,* turns a style of Naipaulian transparency and rigor on the latest passengers to India, circling around an Indian student who's never been outside his homeland.

Ghosh's sweeping historical novel, *The Glass Palace,* begins with a young boy watching the British stormy the Burmese royal fortress in 1885. Eleven year old Rajkumar, an impoverished orphan from India, Sneaks into the forbidden place and meets Dolly, a beautiful young court attendant. Amid the Chaos of looting and violence, Dolly's face is permanently etched into Rajkumar's memory. Soon after, Dolly follows the banished king and queen to India, while Rajkumar stays in Burma, making his fortune in the timber industry. The young man is haunted by Dolly until years later, when he meets her again in India. *The Glass Palace* traces the story of their love during the tumultuous 20th Century. Ghosh grounds his work in the unassailable march of history and the unpredictable swings of fate, infusing his novel with a sense of the tragic. History is more than a backdrop for the story of Dolly's and Rajkumar's lives; it is a powerful force that constantly threatens and dwarfs each individual in-the novel. All of Ghosh's characters struggle through an almost overwhelming number of turbulent event. British imperialism, depression, world war II, the Japanese invasion of Burma and Malaya, India's struggle for independence, and military rule in Myanmar. As in his previous work, Ghosh interweaves several intricate plot lines that follow the lives of multiple characters. But The Glass Palace is even more ambitious in the territory it attempts to cover; the story of three generations of three families in Burma, Malaya and India. Therefore in the views of Frederick Luis Aidama:

"Amitav Ghosh continues to explore different storytelling forms and to complicate the picture of pre- and postcolonial South Asian identity in his fourth novel, *The Glass Palace.* Ghosh's ambitious epic tells the stories of a cast of characters, royal, working- clags, and bourgeois Indians, Bengalis, and Burmese - as they grapple with their sense of place and self while violent historical events reshape twentieth century Burma and India". [2001: 132-133]

The Glass Palace is about geographical entities, space, distance and time. Many stories have been woven together. There are many characters. It is a Saga of many families, their lives and their connection with each other. *The Glass Palace,* is the story of an Indian orphan Rajkumar. Who is transported to Burma by accident. Rajkumar the boy who is eleven years old is remarkable for his exploring spirit, keen perception and his ability to take calculated risks. He works in tea stall of a matronly lady Ma Cho. He loves exaggerating his age just of feel like an adult. He is established as bold, and remarkable. Once Rajkumar lands in Mandalay, his life long search for places and people begins. He is taken in by the city:

> "When the fort's full immensity revealed itself, Rajkumar came to a halt in the middle of the road. The citadel was a miracle to behold, with its mile-long walls and its immense moat. The crenellated ramparts were almost three storeys high, but of a soaring lightness, red in colour, and topped by ornamented gateways with seven tired roof. Long straight roads radiated outwards from the walls, forming a neat geometrical grid. So intriguing was the ordered pattern of these streets that Rajkumar wandered far a field, exploring". [5]

And Rajkumar is a complete destitute in an alien city

with absolutely no acquaintances. Finally, he goes to Ma Cho for job and Ghosh described the outer appearance of Ma Cho -

> "Ma Cho was small and harried looking, with spirals of wiry hair hanging over her forehead, like a fringed awaning. She was in her mid-thirties, more Burmese than Indian in appearance". [5-6]

At Mandalay, he is helping Ma Cho to run a dhaba just outside the royal palace. He gets curious about the fort, therefore he asked Ma Cho regarding the fort and Ma Cho had seen the fort's part inside and she says :

> "It's very large, much larger than it looks. It's a city in itself, with long roads and canals and gardens. First you come to the house of officials and noblemen. And then you find yourself in front of a stockade, made of huge teakwood posts. Beyond lie the apartments of the Royal Family and their servants hundred and hundred of rooms, with gilded pillars and polished floors. And right at the centre there is a vast hall that is like a great shaft of light, with shinning crystal walls and mirrored ceiling. People call it The Glass, Palace." [7]

At the outset of the novel readers are given a brief glimpse of the palace through the awe-struck eyes of a eleven year old Urchin as it was being sacked and plundered by the local people before the British takeover. The Glass Palace is Symbolic of power as well as fragility of imperialism. It was the dazzling emblem of the country's elegance and self-sufficiency until devastated by the British rule. In *The Glass Palace* 'Glass Palace' functions as a metaphor, Glass is brittle and implies transparency. Palace is the symbol of power. Glass palace is an illusion that is created around power. The people in the glass palace do not have the liberty to throw stones at others. The colonized people are always imprisoned in the glass palace and they have lost the capacity to throw stones at the colonial masters. The more the colonized attempt to describe the colonizer's exploitation and violence, the more they reflect on the colonizer's complicity with the colonizer's ideology. The colonized have lost the capacity to speak on their own.

After the initial description of the palace, which gives the novel its title. A little before the end of the novel one comes across a young researcher of Rangoon University writing a dissertation on a famous nineteenth century history of Burma called *The Glass Palace, Chronicles* –

> "The young girl who'd helped to Shelter Dinu when he'd passed through Rangoon in 1942. She was now doing in her mid-twenties, a student at Rangoon University. She was doing research in Burmese literature, writing a dissertation on The Glass Palace Chronicles a famous nineteenth century history, written in the reign of King Bodawpaya, an ancestor of King Thebaw's". [532]

Dolly's Son Dinu, one of the survivors in this vast saga of intertwing families runs a modest photo studio "The Glass Palace" where young people, stifled by the military dictatorship of present day Burma, gather to open their minds to discuss books, pictures and ideas. Needless to say that the symbolism of the title is not laboured. Without making an added effort, Ghosh is able to imbue the title with the images of loss as well as hope. Almost all Amitav Ghosh's novels invariably focus on history and its ramification across geography, a theme that has seldom been explored before and which he does so well with his creative imagination equipped with his own another topological training. His luminous prose matches the inventiveness of his narrative. Here Ghosh makes no attempt to be lyrical or evocative in style as always avoiding the staging of subaltern speech he writes in the unadorned grapholet what comes alive before us is the clear lucid narrative vividly concretized characters, their desires longings and ambition constantly swayed and disrupted by the tide of history But the blending of the public and the personal sphere is seamless and perfect.

As Ghosh tells, 'a cloud of dust' tends to hang over the colonial scenario. Whole cities are on the run and it is often impossible to 'See far', given the panicky conditions. Under the circumstances, then, it is not surprising that Ghosh also uses, the metaphor of the camera to slow events down to pace where it is actually possible to focus. The glass palace of his title, it turns out, indicates both the magnificent hall of mirrors, which forms the centrepiece of the Mandalay residence of Burmese kings and the name of a 'Small photo studio' where the book's action appropriately ends.

> "But you have an address for him then?' Jaya said. 'Yes; Ilongo reached into his pocket and took out a sheet of paper. 'He has a small photo studio, Does portraits, wedding pictures, group photographs. That short of thing. The address is for his studio: he lives right above it".
>
> "He held the paper out to her and she took it. The sheet was smudged and crumpled. She peered at it closely, deciphering the letters. The first words that met her eyes were: The Glass Palace: Photo Studio". [502]

Fiction, at its best provides us with 'addresses' for the lost actors in the historical chronicle. By dwelling on small details and bestowing on ordinary lives an attention that the historical stricter animals cannot afford, a writer creates an interior history such an internalized record of emotions runs parallel to explicit factual accounts and fills them out, At this elusive juncture so to speak story meets history and makes it a little more comprehensible Agenre like the novel especially is suited to the task of bringing content back to those empty frames from which the colonial subject is always vanishing.

Like Ilongo a novelist reaches into his pocket and holds

out his smudged and crumpled sheet of paper so that the recorder can 'decipher it in a manner that combines facts with effect photographic accuracy with the uncertainties of memory that is why I can not think of a clutch of sentences which better describe Ghosh's own labours in this massive 547 page novel than these. "He has a small photo-studio. Does wedding pictures, group photographs. That sort of thing" It would be quite accurate to say that wedding and group portraits from the bulk of the matter in *The Glass Palace.* Ghosh's technique is simply to borrow the warournalist's tripod, lenses and so forth, and then swivel his viewfinder so that it alights on families living out heir lives in tumultuous times.

Saya John comes closest to what Rajkumar could have called a father. But this does not come in a day. Rajkumar matures fast. Life teaches him its own lessons. At him heart, he is always certain about his success in life. When the British throw down the king of Burma, Rajkumar is told that the British wish to control Burmese territory for wood. And from this point starts his shaping of his future plans. He senses wealth in teak. When the city is rampaged by the British, it is the Indian soldiers who come on orders of their colonial masters. Suddenly Indians become the target of mob frenzy. Rajkumar is also attacked. He is saved by Saya John. That day, Saya perceives something unique in Rajkumar. There was something unusual about the boy, a kind of watchful determination. No excess of gratitude here, no gifts or offerings, no talk of honour, with murder in heart. There was no simplicity in his face, no innocence; his eyes were filled with worldliness, curiosity, and hunger. That was as it should be. Saya John is a fine example of this breed of hybridity. His clothes are western. He speaks English, Hindustani and Burmese. His face looks like that of Chinese. Saya himself makes fun of his amalgamated identity:

> "The soldiers there were mainly Indians and they asked me this very question: how is it that you, who

look Chinese and carry a Christian name, can speak our language? When I told them how this had come about, they would laugh and say, you are dhobiKaKutta - a washerman's dog- na ghar Ka na Ghat Ka - you don't belong anywhere, either by the water or on land, and I'd say, Yes, that is exactly what I am. He laughed, with an infectious hilarity, and Rajkumar Joined in". [10]

This is laughter of mutual sharing. Rajkumar is as much a washerman's dog as Saya John. There is no humiliation between the two. This is simple acceptance of fact.

From Rajkumar, the novel expands to a vast array of characters in Burma, India and Malaya, all connected through the broader currents of history and the intimate links of friendship and marriage out of this large cast, the two most searing portraits are of Rajkumar, the unquestioning empire builder, and Arjun, the tormented warrior who tries desperately to break free of the empire that has molded him.

In the 19th century, Britain was expanding its commercial interests, especially in its colonies. India in particular had become not just a continent to exploit and rule, but a source of raw labour and military muscle that bolstered British dominance worldwide and kept the imperial machine humming. With the end of slavery in the empire in 1833, Thousands of poor, willing Indian workers were recruited for work in Burma, Fiji, the Caribbean and Africa, on plantation, in docks, mills and railroads, while others were conscripted into the British army, turning India into what one character in *The Glass Place* calls a 'Vast garrison'.

This is the complicated backdrop from Ghosh's novel, which centers on the fascinating story of Indians in Burma, By the late 19th century, there was a sizable Indian community in Burma; many were recruited to fill the lowly positions; others, such as Rajkumar, came to prosper as merchants in the growing economy. In the 20th Century, as India's independence movement gained strength, and England and Japan faced off in East Asia, these overseas Indians stood at a particularly agonizing crossroads, which tested their sense of national identity. Tragically, the idyll of Indian families in Burma ended in 1942, during the Japanese invasion, when thousands were forced to flee by foot through Jungle and mountains back to India.

Rajkumar is the quintessential opportunist, in the best sense of the word. He makes his first money recruiting in indentured workers in India, then builds up a teak export business in the hills of Burma. Through Rajkumar we can observe the wheels of British commerce transforming the subcontinent and its other colonies into a vast network of trading and exploitation. And though this book aims at a deep critique of empire, Ghosh does not have so narrow an agenda as to simply bash the imperial masters. After all, in the new colonial system, someone like Rajkumar is not stuck in his born station in life, but given a greater chance to succeed on his own initiative. Instead, through the novel's characters, Ghosh shows the subtle questions of allegiance that come to torment them all.

The initial impulse for a colonial enterprise, as is well known, is often commercial, leading to the establishment of a trading post or some such outfit. Thus, it is the Burmese teak and the Malayan rubber that spur the British colonial drive. With a prescience beyond his years, the seven year old Mathew reports to his unbelieving friend Rajkumar what his father, Saya John, has told him, namely, that the English:

> "Want all the teak in Burma. The King won't let them have it so they're going to do away with him". [15]

Once the colonial power is firmly established and has a clear military superiority over the hapless and unprepared native rulers, it looks for, and often fabricates, a dispute with an inconvenient native ruler so as to justify dethroning him, annexing his state, and sending him into exile. A dispute with a British timber company, in which the company was clearly in the wrong, it was used as an excuse for waging a war against king Thebaw in Mandalay. One of the King's senior ministers -

> "had suggested discreetly that it might be best to accept the terms, that the British might allow the Royal Family to remain in the palace in Mandalay, on terms similar to those of the Indian princes - like farmyard pigs in other words, to be fed and fattened by their masters, swine, housed in sties that had been tricked out with a few little bits of finery". [21-22]

But the fiery queen contemptuously turns down the suggestion. The colonial powers usually win not because their cause is just but because of superior power, manipulative skill, and weaponry. The second dimension is the conquest of Burma at the hands of colonized Indians. This conquest took place at various levels -

> "There were some ten thousand soldiers in the British invasion force and of these the great majority- about two thirds were Indian sepoys". [26]

Rajkumar, who worked in a Burmese food stall before the conquest, catapults into prosperity. He lures men and women from India and makes a fortune out of indenturing them in Burma. What Ghosh achieves in this novel is probably what he was hinting at when he suggested how a writer would deal with so much violence in our times. It would be interesting to see how this perspective, making its appearance at this Juncture merely as the ghost of a shadow, gradually concretizes into the real things as we move through the novel. Here, Saya John throws some more light on the phenomenon of Indian soldiers constituting the British army. When he was working as an orderly in a hospital in Singapore, Saya John came across several wounded Indian soldiers who were in their twenties. It was the money that drew them to this profession. Yet what they earned was a few annas a day, not much more than a dockyard coolie. He is certain that:

> "Chinese peasants would never do this-allow themselves to be used to fight other people's wars with so little profit for themselves". [29-30]

Amitav Ghosh refers to the phrase "banality of evil" in the context of soldiers fighting for their British masters from neither enmity nor anger, but in submission to orders from superiors, without protest and without conscious. The process of colonization and the state of the colonized are very relevant thought components of this novel. The very word used Rajkumar *Koala* is objectionable, which is decolorized at least in the actual process of aggression, capture and colonization. How the Burmese people are robbed of all grace with guns and artillery. The British are only giving commands.

Rajkumar is an orphan has an immigrant's characteristic Knack for carving a niche in an alien world. It is through his eyes that we witness the humiliation of King Thebaw and his chief consort queen. Soldiers loot the palace reassured by the ramblings of the Queen that her defeat is not complete –

> "Through all the years of the Queen's reign the towns folk had hated her for her cruelty, feared her for her ruthlessness and courage. Now through the alchemy of defeat she was transformed in their eyes. It was as though a bond had been conjured into existence. That had never existed before. For the first time in her reign she had become what a sovereign should be, the proxy of her people". [34]

Rajkumar catches a fateful glimpse of Dolly, one of the Queen's maids. Through the intertwing stories of Dolly and the Rajkumar, the history of the twentieth century is told. Wars or fought, rebellions are discussed, and fortunes are made and lost. The writer reports everything like a thoughtful, competent, dispassionate and precise observer and his observations are backed up by a meticulous research. Rajkumar gradually succeeds in becoming with the loyal help of his friends Doh Say, Saya John and others, a rich and respected member of the Indian community in Burma. Thereafter, he tracks down Dolly, devoted maid of Queen Supalayat, with whom he had fallen in love at first sight as a boy during the British takeover of Mandalay, Dolly now lives in the distant Indian city of Ratanagiri where she has made a lifelong friend of Uma, the unruly wife of the Indian District commissioner assigned to 'took after' King Thebaw and his family. Through Uma's good offices, Rajkumar finally gets to marry Dolly. All this happens by the end of chapter sixteen. The rest of the chapters of *The Glass Palace,* during a period of history both harrowing and exciting, the interaction between three families, of Dolly and Rajkumar in Burma, of Uma and her brother in India and of Saya John - Rajkumar's mentor, and his son Matthew in Malaysia. Rajkumar once told Uma earlier in their lives when they were young and sensible.

> "Have you ever built anything? Given a single person a Job? Improved anyone's life in any way? No. All you ever do is stand back, as though you were above all of us, and you criticize and criticize. Your husband was as fine a man as any I've ever met, and you hounded him to his death with your self-righteousness". [248]

The truth of these lines is self-evident. Even with these bitterly true words Uma does not go into any kind of self questioning, well, all that one can say is that this amounts to a flaw to draw a character who is a celebrated international socialite and intellectual and yet who never goes into any kind of introspection. Uma's characterization looks unreal. Even to the crudest woman, widowhood drives into bouts of loneliness and depression. The endless Vacuum of life pervades their personality. How can an educated, sensitive, patriotic, modern lady escape an inevitable thought process?

The novel is divided into seven parts and each section highlights the important aspects of the novel. The first part is called Mandalay. It is here that the novel begins and it depicts how the British occupied Burma. The second section is entitled 'Ratanagiri where the calamitous effects of imperialism are shown. The third section, 'The Money Tree' shows how Rajkumar prospers through timber business. The fourth section deals with the second generation. Rajkumar's son, Neel marries Manju and people like Arjun and Dinu show fascination for the British. The fifth section 'Morningside depicts the consequences of Second World War in Malaya. The penultimate section depicts how characters suffer due to the outbreak of the Second World War. The last section of the novel, also entitled 'The Glass Palace' deals with the peak of Indian National Movement and its final achievement of independence.

To Arjun 'modern' and 'western' are synonymous. To become a 'modern India' and western are synonymous. To become a modern India he was prepared to erase all traces of being Indian, discard his past and embrace western habits of thought in its totality. At this stage he does not realize the cost he would be paying to be accepted as a member of the elitist class, the rulers' class this sense of euphoria he was reveling in is partially shattered when he comes to attend his sister's marriage. The motley crowd of politicians, congressmen, Buddhist monks, Burmese student activist, all the invitees to the wedding had nothing but sneer for these men in uniform. The congressmen, who had bitter memories of their confrontation with Indian Soldiers and police, berate Arjun for serving in an army of occupation. Arjun retorts:

> "'We aren't occupying the country" as lightly as he could. 'We are here defend you,' 'From whom are you defending us? From ourselves? From other Indians? It's your masters from whom the country needs to be defended". [287-88]

This is exactly the reply of an officer who has been indoctrinated in the western ideology. He has meticulously internalized the teachings of the British. The young Indian officer has great respect for his superiors in the Army, and aping their statements, behaviour and manner has become his habit. Dressed in western clothes, he has become a man with a black skin but white mask, mentally. Such is his fascination for the army that he does not, even for a moment, reflects upon the inscription at the military academy at Dehradun. This inscription in the military academy should have actually set Arjun thinking about what he was doing. That he was not serving his country does not occur to him even at that point. This is because the British by that time had managed to create a halo about their goodwill.

The first real stirrings of disquiet occur in the transitional figure of Beni Prasad Dey, the district collector responsible for the welfare of the King of Burma, who was exiled to Ratanagiri in India. The collector, as he is known in the Glass Palace, has achieved the ultimate status for an Indian, as an esteemed civil servant in the bureaucratic Raj. And yet the collector is plagued by doubts, "haunted by the fear of being thought lacking by his British collector is confronted with the awkward position of being a willing servant to an alien power.

By the beginning of the 20th Century, the British Empire had evolved from being a powerful trading presence into a huge government apparatus, imposing its hierarchies and protocols on its colonies. Figures such as the collector were instrumental in enforcing its myriad colonial rules, even the most absurd ones, such as treating the kind of Burma like a caged animal and controlling who his daughters, the princesses, could marry. As the collector's wife, Uma, reflects, "Did this mean that one day all of India would become a shadow of what it had been? Millions of people trying to live their lives in conformity with incomprehensible rules?" The collector, a tragic figure, is seeded with an incipient nationalism one that is thwarted by time and place.

A generation later in the late 1930s, Arjun, the nephew of Uma, takes the self-questioning to new, agonizing heights. Arjun Joins the British Army and becomes one of the first Indian officers to rise in its ranks, At first as a colonized subject, even eating at the officer's mess hall was an exhilarating barrier to smash, Arjun is venturing where few Indians had ever gone, mingling with Englishmen and talking and behaving like them, too. If the west represented progressive modernism, Arjun throws himself headlong into this frontier in the hopes of turning himself into a "new, more complete kind of Indian". Eventually, though, the slights of the British officers and the rumblings of dissatisfaction among fellow Indian soldiers who question the Crown's aims when their own cause, freedom has been delayed trouble Arjun.

In the Indian epic the *Mahabharata,* Arjun is the warrior who pauses in battle to question the purpose of war and the kingdom he is fighting for. So too does this modern Arjun begin to doubt his soldier's training- during World War II, when he encounters those drawn to the aims of the Indian National Army.

As a fellow soldier, 'it was strange to be sitting on one side of a battle line, knowing that you had to fight and knowing at the same time that it wasn't really your fight'. During the Japanese invasion, Arjun comes to understand what it means to literally give over his trained body in bloody battle, and he wonders whether he even possesses his own self. He sees himself as molded by 'Unseen potter, he had become a thing unto itself, no longer aware of the pressure of the potter's hand. Worse yet, in surrendering himself so completely to the British army, he realizes that he had never acted of his own Volition, never had a moment of true self-consciousness'. He had become an unthinking machine, well-oiled and well-trained to fight for the Crown. 'Everything he has ever assumed about himself was a lie, an illusion.' He was sacrificing his very life, and yet this life was no longer his own.

In the narrative that follows, we go back with Rajkumar and Dolly to Rangoon, where he, though Scarcely literate, sets up a booming business in timber, and we see one of their sons Neel, become a film producer and the other, Dinu, a photographer. At the same time we follow Dolly's best friend Uma, who, when her civil servant husband dies, takes off for Europe and then in flight from its "ruthless hypocrisies", to New York where she joins a group of Indians who agitate for independence under the tutelage of Irish activists. The novel has many windows virtual and actual but Uma independent minded to the end, is the strongest of them all. While Rajkumar tries to turn even war into an occasion for profit, she returns to India to spread the word of Burma's suffering and to Join Gandhi in his nonviolent fight for freedom.

In an author's note at the end of the novel *The Glass Palace*, Ghosh refers to a "near obsessive urge to render the backgrounds of my characters' lives as closely as I could" and it is this urge that is often most evident throughout the novel. He has consulted "hundreds of books, memoirs," and we get, for example, fascinatingly detailed accounts of how teak camps worked in the Burmese Jungle or how rubber plantation tappers began their day in Malaya. At times the research almost swallows up the story; we are treated to a brief excursus on the delights of Nyonya food and we learn that the current way of wearing a Sari, with blouse and petticoat, was in fact the invention of an Indian official during the Raj. At one point Ghosh suddenly begins classifying cars, and we realize, perhaps with alarm, that this is a device comparable to the flapping of calendar pages in old movies, to show where we are in time.

The real heart of the novel, though, and its dramatic centerpiece, lies in the classic imperial setting of World War Second in Burma and Malaya, here everything that is powerful in Ghosh's somewhat aerial perspective, and everything that in shaky, comes to the fore. He takes us into the Southeast Asian theater of war by cutting back and forth between a shy romance on a rubber plantation in Malaya's highlands, a microcosm of empire and another involving the Indian soldiers who are fighting for the British as the Japanese approach. In the love scenes, the wide screen approach leads to some curious effects. As Dinu, the photographer, lies with his beloved, he watches "the horizontal planes of her forehead, her eyebrows and her mouth perfectly balanced by the verticals of her black, straight hair and the translucent filaments that hung suspended from her lips." The man sees life through camera angles, to be sure, but still it seems odd that the closer the bodies get. The more abstract the language becomes.

Yet even as he seems somewhat ill at case here with intimacy, and so squanders the emotional force of the scene. Ghosh conveys the larger picture with particular vividness. We see Christians tree in the department stores of Rangoon whose branches are "whitened with a frosting of culticur a talcum powder," and as the Japanese move through Malaya, we follow great crowds of people running for evacuation trains only to find that all the cars are reserved for Europeans. The road's embankment was dotted with parked vehicles. Families could be seen to be sleeping in their cars, snatching a little rest before day light. At intervals one and a half ton military trucks came barreling down the highway, heading south.

Typical of everything that is most affecting in *The Glass Palace* are the passages evoking the panicked exodus of tens of thousands of people, nearly all of then Indian, as the Japanese took over Burma in 1942. Even those lucky enough to have made it to Calcutta, more than a thousand miles away, arrived in an already impoverished city in the throes of one of the worst faminesin its history. In some ways the two themes that have animated Ghosh's writing from the beginning his interest in the lives of middle class Indian families and his concern for the world's afflicted, come together stirringly as the very people who once thrived in Burma suddenly turn into dispossessed refugees themselves, struggling across rivers and mountains, wheeling the elderly in carts and often dying along the way. The worlds of his fiction and of his reportage memorably converge.

The scene that Ghosh enters most intensely, though, and that seems nag at him with unusual force, is the one involving Uma's easy going nephew, Arjun, who prides himself on becoming one of the first Indian officers in the British army, even as the Indians around him begin asking ever more impatiently why they're risking their lives to protect the very people who are holding them down. As the novel goes on, more and more of them begin slipping away to join the Indian National Army, the unfortunate group that joined the Japanese only to find that its Eastern masters were no more solicitous of its members' interests than its western ones had been over and over we return to the intense discussions among the solders as Ghosh argues with great sympathy that the Indians who might be reflexively written off as "collaborators" were in fact confused idealist ready to do anything to fight for freedom from British oppression. He also tells us intriguingly in his another note that his father was one of the "loyal Indians" who fought with the British throughout often against the Indians defectors These characters torn between two kinds of oppression traitors if they supports the British traitors if they turn to ward the Japanese take Ghosh back to what has always seemed to be his central concern the consequences of displacement and his exhaustive research here excavate the many ironies of a British system ready to go through the motions of offering Indians powers yet not really willing to change deep down Indian soldiers were discouraged from carrying umbrellas he tells because they were a traditionalizing of sovereignty. Dinner jackets were customarily worm at the mess on Thursdays, "This being the day of the week when the news of queen Victoria's death had been received in India".

Ghosh treats all but a few of his characters with tenderness yet it soon becomes clear that the ones he regards as the most treacherous are the ones who collaborated with the British, aping the very people who looked down on them, and in this book at least, nearly always destroyed by the empire they served. At one point Arjun, who has grown more and more troubled by his service to the British army, abruptly kills his most loyal attendant to save him from the plight of becoming an Indian with divided loyalties. Arjun recognizes that he doesn't believe in the collective promise. For him, it's his personal sense of betrayal that makes him do what he does. He discovers in the course of this narrative is that he had imagined himself to be something that he was not. He had seen himself in a certain way, and then he comes to realize that what he saw himself as was a lie. It's not nationalism for him. For his friend Hardayal, it is the promise of truth and duty and freedom, Arjun explicitly does not believe in any of this. For him, it's entirely the idea that he has been formed and shaped by the manipulative hand in such a way that he himself has ceased to understand who he is or what he is. It's the unbearable pain of this that makes him do what he does.

At the outset, Arjun takes cover under the belief that soldiering is a Job and he was trying to do it as best as he could. However, a series of disturbing events keep battering on the schism that has set in now, so that it eventually bursts into decisive action on the part of Arjun. The antiwar protest march taken out by the congressmen initiates a debate among Dinu, Arjun and Uma when they were on their way home from shopping in Kolkatta. The debate revolves round the question of wisdom in choosing in the context of world war second one evil over the other the imperialist British on the one hand and the Fascist and the racist Germany and Militant Japan on the other Dinu maintains that Hitler and Mussolini are among the most tyrannical and destructive leaders in all of human history. That India and Burma will not be any better off if the British are defeated because the German rule will be more violent and despotic than the British. He mentions the ruthless massacre of Jews by the Germans. Uma counters this argument stating that the expansionist aspirations of Germany and Japan can be traced to the successful imperialist British model. She says the British Empire is equally guilty of killing tens of millions of people in its conquest of the World, in its appropriation of the entire continents. Greater good, she seems to believe, will be done, if the model is demolished. Dinu draws Uma's attention to the evils like caste system, untouchability, widow burning, etc. That were prevalent in India even before the British came and asks why talk about the evils of the Empire. Uma is quick to respond stating that the Indian struggle for independence is not separated from their struggle for reform. Colonialists, she tells Dinu, would like us to believe this, but that is an absolute lie -

> "It is true that India is driven with evils such as those you describe - caste, the mistreatment of women, ignorance, illiteracy. But take the example of your own country, Burma - they had no caste system there. - It is simple mistaken to imagine that colonialist sit down and ponder the rights and wrongs of the societies they want to conquer: that is not why empires are built". [294-295]

Uma points out that the Indian nationalists also do not sympathize with the Nazis and the Fascists. The novel reveals in clear terms how tactfully and shrewdly the British have conquered countries and subjugated whole populations, exiling Kings to erase them completely from public memory at home. Ghosh pinpoints the resistance to the dictatorial military rule in the postcolonial Burma through some student activist's arguments about the atrocities of dictators like Hitler and Mussolini in Dinu's photo studio called The Glass Palace in Rangoon. Beside power politics, the Indian diasporic experience in South East Asia is the focal point and Ghosh records its historical depth and meaning in the novel. Several stories of expatriates and exiles mingle and Jostle with the interaction of class race, gender and religion in it. Rajkumar who is infatuated with Dolly Sein, as beautiful as The Glass Palace itself, marries her and ventures into the rubber plantation industry as Saya John's partner. Rajkumar's life story is a story of the struggle for survival in the colonial turmoil. As a colonized subject from Bengal, he becomes a colonizer in Burma transporting indentured labourers from South India to other parts of the colonial world. He has even sexually exploited a woman worker on his plantations. His postcolonial consciousness represents a conflict within his own self, a conflict through which he tries to step outside his colonial self, the history of the imperial phase and to approach his own past, history and reality from his present position.

As a person of serious attitudes, Dinu's fall in love is also very intentional and possessive business. We cannot say that he is totally successful here. His attraction for Alison is absolute. But once Arjun, Uma's nephew who is serving in Indian army, enters the scene, the equilibrium is lost. The liveliness of Alison matches with Arjun's power and for a short span of time Dinu loses Alison to Arjun. He is Jealous of Arjun and his loud impressive ways. He tries to come to terms with the situation. He knows that Alison cannot be trusted with Arjun. But he just cannot do anything about it. He has only his inner resources. He decides not to fall a prey to self pity. Alison, on the other hand, comes to the conclusion that between Dinu and Arjun there hardly exists any comparison. Her analysis provides a beautiful picture of these two men. This shows Ghosh's art of typical type of characterization -

> "'Arjun - you're not in charge of what you do; you're a toy, a manufactured thing, a weapon in someone else's hands. Your mind doesn't inhabit you body', - She saw that despite the largeness and authority of his presence, he was a man without resources, a man whose awareness of himself was very slight and very fragile, she saw that Dinu much stronger and more resources". [376]

The Glass Palace performs an invaluable service in showing us how the events of the last century, and especially the war, looked to many people in Burma and India, whose voices have seldom been heard before in the west, but its narrative is observed occasionally by an abundance of detail, occasionally by political argument. History is more than whispers in the background in *The Glass Palace*. When the Japanese invade Burma, for example, the character lives crumble. Not of course, before characters like Arjun and Dolly experience moments of life changing awareness. Dolly finds deep spirituality as an unguent to Rajkumar's in humane, exploitative business ways. Arjun's firsthand experience with the horror and hypocrisies of war shakes him to the core. 'If it were true that his life had somehow been molded by acts of power of which he was unaware, then it would follow that he had never acted of his own volition, never had a moment of true self consciousness. Everything he had ever assumed about himself was a lie, an illusion. Ghosh's inquiry loses its focus, however, as Arjun alternates accounts of passionate sex on beaches and in forests with set pieces about battle and migrations. It is as if Ghosh's very Naipaulian urge to examine the deception of self-deceptions of the colonized mind had been held in check by his ambition to write a big historical novel with a multiplicity of characters and settings and themes. The novelist scrambles to cover too many bases at once; the result is that ideas as well as dramatic situations often feel hastily imposed from above.

When, at the end, Ghosh abruptly provides a primer on contemporary Burmese polities, and has one of his hastily improvised characters meet Daw Aung San Suukyi, the most famous opponent of Myanmar's military regime, and declare that it is 'impossible to behold this woman and not be half in love' it becomes impossible not to behold the author himself in transparent disguise, indeed, Ghosh has written admiringly about Aung Sun Suukyi in the New Yorker. On the last page, the bedroom scene between Rajkumar and Uma, the two aged survivors of

War and destruction, feel equally rushed in dramatizing the over used idea of sexual love as redemption from history - an idea also present on the last page of Ghosh's aesthetically more satisfying *novel Shadow Lines.*

> "They woke up, blinking short sighted. They were both extremely short sighted and there ensued a flurry of bed shaping and pillow turning as they fumbled for their eyeglasses. In the process, their covers slipped off and their bodies were revealed to be naked. Urna's skin looked very soft and was covered with a delicate tracery of tiny cracks, every single hair on Rajkumar's body had turned white, creating a startlingly elegant effect against his dark complexion". [546]

Even, the pathos of Arjun's death is somewhat muffled in the din of murders and suicides and historical events Ghosh has to create in order to achieve resolution. Arjun dies fighting for an unwinnable cause, condemned to nihilism by his self-awareness, his quickening sense of his intellectual and emotional infirmities. The last scene of the novel is a monument that strange human complexity that was missing in so many other places. .

The Glass Palace brings together history, fiction, autobiographical records and memories. Ghosh has stated that the "issue of how the past is to be remembered lies at the heart of *The Glass Palace"* in his letter to the Commonwealth Foundation, wherein hc withdrew the novel trom being considered for an award. The letter expresses the author's feeling that -

> "I would be betraying the spirit of my book if I were to allow it to be incorporated within that particular memorialization of the Empire that posses under the rubric of 'the commonwealth'". [*The Indian Review of Books* : 2001]

Ghosh's letter indicates one of the directions in which history is to be remembered. The colonial experience and its memories are loaded with a sense of pain and suffering of the large numbers of people who lived through those phases of history.

In reconstructing the history of Burma's transition from a kingdom to a republic, between 1885 to 1995 - the period covered by *The Glass Palace,* Ghosh has used material derived from a variety of sources - recollections and remembered accounts of his father, uncle and several other living persons who he met; the diaries, notes and official records; history books etc. However, Ghosh calls *The Glass Palace* "unqualifiedly a novel", "a wholly fictional world". [549] History is woven into fiction and an epical saga of the colonial regime in Burma and India is created. Bound in the shared colonial situation the two people look at each other, relate and mix, and, then separate, constructing images of the 'self and the 'other'. Localized contexts of India and Burma become the sites of self-consciousness, self-enquiry and a process of recovering the lost self hood. Ghosh seeks an understanding of the past to have a bearing upon the present. The past is remembered not as a dead, remote period, but as flowing on, into the present, postcolonial situations of multi-ethnic, pluralist societies, of boundaries and mutations of nations imposed by the colonial rulers and complex cultural diversities of a persistent political struggle for democratic and egalitarian system. Ghosh uses his position as a 'specular' border - intellectual, as Abdul Jan Mohammed [1995: 441] has defined in his essay "Worldliness without World, Homelessness as Home", an intellectual who is located on the outside / margin, and seeks to analyze understand his society from that position.

Amitav Ghosh's novel *The Glass Palace* is one of the few novels to relate India and Burma in the shared colonial experience, during which a new sense of selfhood and national identity took shape among the people of the two countries. Crossing the borders between the two countries historical characters like King Thebaw and his family and purely fictional characters like Raj Kumar, Dolly, Saya John and Uma reflect upon the historical events and their impact upon the colonized people. The novel moves across genres of writing as well, bringing together fiction and autobiography cultural, social and political histories, as it explores a century of Indian history, of Burma's movement from 'Kingdom to Republic' [Frank Trager: 1966:39], a journey that is still going on.

The Glass Palace begins with the deposition of King Thebaw, the last of Burma's kings. With his removal from the Glass Palace inside the fabulous Mandalay Fort, monarchy came to an abrupt end, and Burma became a part of the British Empire in India. Bound together in colonial subjugation the two countries and their people could never come together. As Amitav Ghosh narrates the stories of the people's reactions to these momentous historical events and changes, he presents the discontent, disapproval of the masses and how they began to see image of themselves reflected in the 'other'. The servility and surrender of the Indians to the British - the Burmese felt was a warning to them to prevent them from going to such extents of surrender to the power of the British colonial masters [3].

The novel builds up many little narratives to present the many voices inside the countries, Burma and India, during the one hundred years of political struggle in the subcontinent. It goes into the complex relationship of interactions and conflicts between the Indians and Burmese, presenting along with it the emergence of a more concrete self-consciousness among the different sections of people.

The new awareness of the self, the consciousness of a more individual and independent self of the particular persons is related to the wider movements for national independence and identity. The personal search is woven into the country's search leading to new images of both.

The changed images of the self are metaphorically presented in the novel through a repetition of the image of "The Glass Palace". This was one of the special sections of the Mandalay fort, where important events take place in the beginning of the novel. Queen Supayalat, the ambitious and most loved wife of King Thebaw, it is suggested in the novel, pushes the country into a war with the British; this particular scene is located in the chamber of the palace where the ceiling is -

> "lined with mirrors. As she [Queen] approached its centre, an army of Supayalats seemed to materialize around her ......". [39]

This description emphasizes the self-centered ambitiousness of the Queen, who wanted to make her husband, King Thebaw, a powerful ruler. Here the myriad images in the mirror of the Queen reflect a narcissistic strain in her character. Political power is completely out of touch with the masses. The descriptions of the mobs running into the palace once the king has been defeated by the British army, the humiliating exit of the King and his family from the city, deserted totally by his courtiers, cut off from the people, that Ghosh gives in the novel reflect the complete separation between the King and the masses. Basing his descriptions on some of the well-known histories of Burma, such as by Frank Trager [1966] and W. S. Desai [1961], Ghosh shows the utter unpreparedness of the King to face the power of the British imperial project in Asia. These images in the mirror reflect an older, closed-in political system, completely inadequate to face the new threat.

In contrast to this, there is, in the last part of the novel another Glass Palace - a photographer's studio which is given this name because the mother of the photographer, Dolly, who happened to be one of the attendants of Queen Supayalat used to talk about this Glass Palace [of the king's fort]. Dinu, the photographer, has put the pictures he has taken of the public places, and of ordinary persons and occasions that interested him, without in any sense trying to impose the image of any one class or group. In his "Glass Palace" the images of ordinary people and their work are reflected, creating a people's palace, a democratic open art gallery.

Between the Glass Palace of King Thebaw and that of Dinu, Burma goes through many significant shifts. When he presents the historical events Ghosh focuses on the men and women working in the streets at the lowest level of the society, to reflect upon the historical panorama, at the incidents occurring around them. Both the historical figures [like King Thebaw, Queen Supayalat] and the fictional ones become observers and reflect upon these incidents. They then ask questions that post-colonial societies are engaged with --the failures of the kings of once strong kingdoms, the role of one subjugated nation in oppressing or enslaving other free nations and the real force behind the management of the British Empire. "Handcuffed to history" as they are, these characters' quest towards the understanding of their world and to gain a new self" makes *The Glass Palace* an absorbing novel. As these persons struggle to gain a sense of subjectivity, to come to terms with the complex interconnections between economic, political and cultural developments in the colonial world, there are significant transformations within them, leading toward changes in the national identities.

Rajkumar is among the most important of these 'reflectors'. He has come to Burma from Chittagong to escape the plague. The 11-year-old boy survives in Mandalay on the bases of a sheer determination to survive. When he watches King Thebaw moving out of the city in an ordinary ox-cart, the rows of Burmese citizens standing on the two sides of the road, kept in their place by the Indian sepoys, the boy is moved to wonder why the Indian sepoys agreed to become accomplices of the British in conquering other free countries. He asks Saya John, an elderly man standing with him, about the role of the Indian army. As the narrator - the author fills in informative data - "There were some ten thousand soldiers in the British invasions force, and of these the great majority - about two third - were Indian sepoys." The units deployed had soldiers from "the Hazara Regiment and 1st Madras Pioneers" [26]. These soldiers had fought for the British in different parts of the world and were the most "handy" and "the most loyal of Britain's foot soldiers" the authors, goes on to say.

Saya John and Rajkumar feel contempt and disgust at the 'loyalty' of these soldiers for their 'masters'. It is not merely the money that holds them; Saya John tells Rajkumar that the sepoys he had met in Singapore in a hospital had earned a few annas a day; that they did not seem to be by nature cruel or insensitive [29]. The hold of the British power perplexes the ordinary, illiterate, innocent boy Raj Kumar, his companion Saya John and also King Thebaw. The king is taken away from Burma to a town in India. On the way he looks through his binoculars, something he was very fond of doing; he watches Indian coolies working on the port in Rangoon and wonders how these people had been compelled to leave their homeland to do menial, dirty jobs in Burma:

> "The British had", he knows, "brought them there, to work in the docks and the mills, to pull rickshaws and empty the latrines. Apparently they couldn't find local people to do these jobs and indeed why would the Burmese do that kind of work" [49].

The King thinks about the general standard of his land with an evident sense of pride -

> "In Burma no one ever starved, everyone knew how to read and write, and land was to be had for the asking. Why should they pull rickshaws and carry nightsoil?" [50]

The image of Indian servility contrasts with the Burmese people's sense of greater independence of spirit, and material well-being. These reflections become mirror images warning the Burmese never to 'fall so low' [49]. King Thebaw is amazed at the great power of the empire that could unsettle and displace such large numbers of people moving them around the world.

He cannot understand this forceful combination of economic, political and military powers - a totally new phenomena for the likes of him - he and Bahadur Shah Zafar. He wonders "what vast, what incomprehensible power" was at play to move people in such large numbers" [50]. Why this "furious movement"? He cannot comprehend the hidden power, the source of energy - of capitalism that has begun to unsettle older systems and is soon going to change his country also completely.

Rajkumar and Saya John move into the teak business rising up slowly and steadily. Through their involvement the dark and ruthless world of the world's 'woodland' is shown. Going into detailed portrayal of the working system of the felling and collecting of mighty teak trees, the novel brings out the loneliness, horror, sickness and hardships of the lives of men engaged in the whole process. White men who came as supervisors were driven by loneliness and sickness to occasional fits of depression, physical and mental breakdown. The driving force of capitalism turns them into 'tools' much as the sepoys had been made the instruments of the Empire. Rajkumar becomes completely absorbed in the capitalistic love for money as an end in itself. First teak, then rubber becomes the object demanded in the new market as automobiles become part of the market. The 'rags to riches' story of Rajkumar and Saya John reflects the real life stories of several Indians who made it big in Burma in the first thirty years of the twentieth century.

This story however has a tragic turn when Burma's nationalist movement turned the Indian into the hated 'outsider' - hated for his greed, exploitation of the raw material and people. Rajkumar is shocked when he realizes he must leave Burma in the 1940s. The 'Long March' back to India once again raises important questions about the nature of national identity, the reality of borderlines between countries and the justification of mass-migrations. Exiles and migrants who moved from one country to another are displaced and become outcastes within their own country and in the new land.

The Glass Palace looks at both the sides of the picture. In the formation of the Burmese sense of national identity, Indian are turned into 'hated outsiders' as a part of their rejection of the British imposition. Rajkumar's long stay in Burma, his marrying Dolly, a Burmese, does not give him a Burmese identity, for he himself had riot cared to acquire such an affiliation. When he comes back to Calcutta, he remains an outsider here too, meeting others like him - reliving in their 'golden' days in Burma.

The Glass Palace portrays several levels of movements and awareness within the colonial period in Burma and India. It is not a one-sided picture of the Burmese perceptions of India's loss of selfhood and fragmentation of the social system. The emergence of a questioning within the Indians, particularly among the middle educated class was an important feature of the process towards the 'recovery' of the sense of selfhood. In the characters of Uma Dey, her husband Bipin Beharey Dey and Arjun, Uma's nephew, Ghosh creates this struggle that developed at a larger scale during the 1920s and 1940s.

Bipin Beharey Dey and Arjun also become aware of their mental subjugation to the imperial racist-oppressive ideology some time after they have been the beneficiaries of its practices that divided the colonized people themselves. At first, Dey and Arjun, who has joined the Indian Army, enjoy the sense of their position in upper strata, in the colonial power structure. But gradually the inherent injustices and falsity of the empires claims of humane liberal civilization purposes are revealed to them and they become disillusioned.

King Thebaw and. Queen Supayalat live in the small town, Ratnagiri; secluded from the major political events of the time. The unjust conditions of the King's exile, complete indifference of the British rulers to the needs of the King as a lawful ruler of a country, as an individual, of the family members, are understood reluctantly by Bipin Beharey who has been made responsible of the King'? veil being. When Bipin Beharey is scandalized by the affair between the elder princess and a poor coachman's son, the Queen retorts that the ill treatment given to the Royal family, their illegal imprisonment are the real, greater scandals. She says "Scandals"?.... The Scandal lies in what you have done to us." The Queen speaks out about the discrepancy between the British claims of having a higher civilization run on the basis of "laws", of justice and fair treatment. She says –

> "..... we have heard so many lectures from you and your colleagues, on the subject of the barbarity of the King of Burma and the humanity of the Angrez.... The English alone understood liberty-; we were told; they do not put kings and prices to death; they rule through the laws. If that is so, why has King Thebaw never been brought to trial?" [149-50]

Bipin Beharey cannot deny the truth of the Queen's charges. He feels ashamed at his helplessness, perceives the immoral nature of his role, as an "officer" of the British government with the sense of a loss in his own self, he chooses death as the only way out.

Arjun discovers his loss of individual identity as he realizes that he has been moulded like a clay-vessel, by the hands of an unknown "potter", to believe in the highly idealistic goal proclaimed by the Empire in modernizing and governing the unruly countries in Asia, and to become a willing 'tool' for that vast power. When he goes to Burma to fight for the British government during the 1940s, he begins to gain the knowledge of his complete submersion into the colonial ideas, as an unthinking, unreflecting – person. A new psychological awareness comes to him from the relationship with Alison, who turns him down saying she felt pity for him rather than love. His friends in the Battalion tell him about the nationalist duties of the Indians and Arjun finds himself caught in a peculiar moral dilemma. The battlefield becomes a ground of Arjun's moral conflict and his first glimpse of a 'self, an inner _core of thinking, feeling and moral responsibility is realized in this conflict of duties towards his country and to the so-called "Masters".

Arjun's painful self-discovery is caught in the complicated history of the Japanese invasion of Burma, their subsequent defeat and the British army's threat of military action against the "deserters" of the British army. Arjun hides in the jungle, hounded more by a sense of shame, of betraying the nation -and his inability to recover the self in a wholesome way. He seeks his death, in the jungle, after killing Kishen Singh, who has stood by him, faithfully.

The Glass Palace creates several 'little' narratives about ordinary persons caught in their personal and inner conflicts and quests. It begins with the portrayal of the King and Queen of Burma, losing their power to an external enemy; towards the end, it creates a completely different image of power and control. It takes the reader to the streets in Burma in the 1990s, leading towards the house of Aung San Suu Kyi, the most popular and perhaps, in a manner, powerful leader of the Burmese people. She holds no political institutional post but has become an institution in herself. Ghosh shows her popularity [541] her openness in facing the public and her ability to laugh. [542]

Timothy Garton Ash [2000: 21-24] in an article on Burma calls Aung San Sui Kyi the "Uncrowned Queen". of Burma and Ghosh also builds up the contrast between the political self-enclosed world of King Thebaw and the deeply loved figure of Aung San, The image of the people's participation and decentralized political movement is vested in the figure of this woman, who does not seek any power or privilege for herself.

In Dinu's Glass Palace, the images of the ordinary life are reflected. The novel *The Glass Palace* presents the decolonization of the images through and in which people think of themselves, understand and conceptualize themselves.-In the last pages of the book Ghosh underscores the fictional aspect of his world. This fictionality of the historical narrative relates the social and existential "reality" of the past to the recollections; past become a "discursive reality" and is used as the referent of art. In Linda Hutcheon's [1988: 24] words "the only 'genuine historicity' becomes that which would openly acknowledge its own discursive, contingent reality'". The "little narratives" become collectively a varied, heterogeneous and many-directional [hi]stories, different from the accounts available in the histories of Burma and, India that Ghosh has consulted. The nation is constructed, perceived through these accounts of the silent and invisible figures living all around the well-known 'historical' figures.

A noticeable aspect of the 'family portraits' mentioned earlier as a characteristic feature of this novel is precisely that they begin with Rajkumar, a young orphan of eleven. To my mind, Rajkumar's sym-bolic as well as real orphan-hood implies that he has to *invent* a family where none exists; he has to build lasting bonds of trust with strangers. Structurally, that is, the unfolding of this novel is associated with the enfolding of family and friends around the central character. As the chief protagonist of Ghosh's novel, that is, Rajkumar has in effect to solve the same dilemma that confronts the postcolonial author. He has actually to *discover his lineage* by achieving creative harmony out of the materials of historical dissension and resentment; and he has to make sense of the 'exit-tential' conundrum that plagues all individuals who cross, for one reason or another, the well-defined lines of 'national identity' and 'family genealogy'.

Were one foolhardy enough to attempt a 175-word summary of *The Glass Palace,* it might go like this: skilled in the art of survival in a difficult world, Rajkumar gradually succeeds in becoming, with the loyal help of his friends Doh Say, Saya John and others, a rich and powerful member of the Indian commu-nity in Burma. Thereafter, he tracks down Dolly, devoted maid of Queen Supalayat, with whom he had fallen in love at first sight as a boy during the British takeover of Mandalay. Dolly now lives in the distant Indian city of Ratnagiri, where she has made a lifelong friend of Uma, the unruly wife of the Indian District Commissioner assigned to 'look after' King Thebaw and his family. Through Uma's good offices, Rajkumar finally gets to marry Dolly. All this happens by the end of Chapter Sixteen. The rest of the forty-eight chapters of *The Glass Palace* concern, during a period of history both harrowing and excit-ing, the interaction between three families: of Dolly arid Rajkumar in Burma, of Uma and her brother in India and of Saya John - Raj-Kumar's mentor - and his son Matthew in Malaysia.

When we first meet Rajkumar he has a temporary job at Ma Cho's tea-shop in Mandalay but just how temporary this position is depends on players much bigger than him: The invasion proceeded so smoothly as to surprise even its planners. The imperial fleet crossed the border on 14 November, 1885 ... A few days later, without informing King Thebaw, the Burmese army surrendered. The war lasted just fourteen days'. In Ghosh's novel, the repercussions of this 'fourteen day war' are tracked for over a century, for the bookends with a snapshot of Aung San Suu Kyi in 1996, the sixth year of her house arrest under the generals.

Writers such as Ghosh have to seek some route other than the magic realist to the realms 'beyond belief that every work of art subliminally demands. *The Glass Palace*, deals with this literary compulsion by incorporating three 'ideal types' within its text, which counterbalance and redeem those brute facts of history that Ghosh is clearly committed to depicting in relentless detail. These are, very simply - the image of perfect but very human beauty in the figures of Dolly and Suu Kyi; the theme of new diasporic beginnings after great upheavals such as the one symbolized by the Burmese royal family's resettlement in Ratnagiri in India or Saya John's son Matthew's creation of the wondrous 'Morning star' plantation in faraway Malay-sia; and finally, the enchantment of criss-crossing coincidences through-out the novel.

Beauty, coincidence and diasporic hope: the three redemptive graces in *The Glass Palace*. I have mentioned the first and last of these already, so it may be time to move on to coincidence now. The psychologist Carl Jung once called coincidence 'the joker in nature's pack of cards' and one sees his point immediately. As he indicated, coincidences were 'synchronous events' which broke the rules of causal determination and invited analysts to probe beyond the certain-ties of everyday reality. Extending these views of Jung's to Ghosh's novel, one could argue that coincidence represents what postmodernists would call an *aporia* or 'break' in the logic of narration, just as post-coloniality marks a disjunction from the earlier trajectory of colonial-ism.

Coincidence, in effect, allows for something like 'fate' or 'the hand of god' to slip into an otherwise down-to-earth historical exposition. Now *The Glass Palace* is not just a thoroughly researched novel, it is a carefully plotted one. This means, that Ghosh goes out of his way to tie up loose ends. *Stylistically,* he is always measured, correct, objec-tive - in the manner of the historian - but *managerially* he isn't altogether able to resist the temptation to play God - in the mode of the novelist. By the time Ghosh reaches the middle of his novel, he has three generations and several families strewn across half the world and must meet the obligation to establish connections between them. He must get his 'group photographs'. Accordingly, Ghosh makes Neel, the elder son of Dolly and Rajkumar appear as if by magic in a Calcutta film-studio all the way from Burma at the exact moment when Manju, the daughter of Uma's brother, is caught in an embarrassing situation. Naturally, Neel rescues Manju and they fall conveniently in love. First coincidence: the neat uniting by marriage of the families of Dolly, the heroine and her best friend Uma.

Another time, Manju's twin brother, Arjun, has his British army unit stationed at the precise location in Malaysia abutting the Morningside estate, leading to his encounter with both Saya John's niece Alison and Rajkumar's son Dinu in one unlikely stroke. Second coincidence: bringing one member each of the second generation of Ghosh's triad of families together in one place, in perfect consonance with Aristotle's traditional injunction that the unities of time and place be observed in any authoritative drama. Still later, having painfully given up his allegiance to the British and crossed over to the Indian National Army, the same Arjun, now emaciated and almost broken, finds himself face-to-face once again with Dinu, since it just so happens that Dinu has been asked to intercede with the INA 'be-cause of his Indian connections'. It stretches one's credulity to believe that of all the exhausted soldiers of the INA, the one to emerge out of the woods is Arjun and the one confronting him his old rival in love and. war, Dinu. But there you have it: coincidence, an unexpected regular in *The Glass Palace*. Coincidence, the irresistible old trickster of fiction, shamelessly asking for a willing suspension of disbelief from the reader - and getting it!

Only a skilled historical novelist can so endear his characters to his audience that they are prepared to 'forget history' from time to time and allow the internal dynamics of the text to dominate events. I have already mentioned that, if a writer's task is to memorialize psychologi-cal space, to correlate invisible inner events with outer experience, this charge carries particular weight in the case of the postcolonial writer. But Ghosh's *The Glass Palace* rises to the challenge with remarkable self-confidence. Despite the novel's bulky package of one hundred years of dates and facts, Ghosh's triumph is that time seldom hangs heavy in the fictional space he has designed for it; and, on several occa-sions, the illusion of restoring an imaginative wholeness to the divided self of colonialism is very successfully maintained via an appeal to luminous concepts like beauty and hope.

In many ways, what is interesting about this millennial novel is how soundly its postcolonial stance rests upon reliably old-fashioned narrative foundations. Family sagas with a sweeping historical back-drop were always a failsafe item in the publishing world - from *The Forsyte Saga* to

Gone with the Wind. The only crucial change to have come about in the past decade or two is that 'the Orient' is now increasingly represented not so much by a Paul Scott or a Pearl S. Buck as by best-selling writers like Jung Chang or Vikram Seth speaking in their 'own' voices. So where have all Scotts and Bucks gone, long time passing? My own hypothesis, hinted at before, is that they comprise the new literary migrants who have moved to a principality adjoining the historical novel - namely, travel writing. Witness the regions now tenanted by Paul Theroux or William Dalrymple. This is because travel-writing is *logically* the province of the 'outsider' and there is thus a certain legitimacy that a writer can claim when he traip-ses off to, say, Ladakh or Somalia or Kandahar, and records his own [mis-]adventures there. In contrast, considerably less sympathy exists, in today's politically correct climate, for the fiction writer who 'appro-priates' the perspective of the 'third-worlder'.

At the same time, new areas of literary discourse like 'postcolonial studies' have ensured, for better or worse, that a certain modicum of world attention is directed towards formations such as the ubiquitous 'Indian Writers in English'. And what has this to do with Ghosh? Well, my contention throughout this essay has been that an 'Indian writer' like Ghosh, who lives in 'the West' but writes about 'elsewhere' is al-most forced today to occupy an inter-generic cusp: between travel-writing, autobiography, informed journalism and fiction. Both Ghosh's *In an Antique Land* [part fictional autobiography; part sociological take on Egypt] and *Dancing in Cambodia, At Large in Burma* [travel-ogue] illustrate this argument perfectly. So does his *Countdown,* on India's 'bomb' [informed journalism]. Other Indian writers in En-glish subject to similar urges and a comparable geographical disloca-tion include both Vikram Seth *[From Heaven Lake]* and Salman Rushdie *[The Jaguar Smile].*

On the whole, Ghosh is a worthy writer, not a scintillating one; and his *The Glass Palace* is important not because it opens new stylistic or thematic doors, but because it reopens old ones so effectively. Burma at the present time is near inaccessible territory; yet Ghosh's book manages to hold up before a global community of readers a historically authen-tic 'golden' Burma as it was – and could be again. At a tune of millen-nial doom, when we are having to radically reconfigure our dimly remembered pasts in order to understand their effects on our chaoti-cally disturbed present, that is the novel's signal postcolonial virtue-elephants, teak, pagodas and all.

WORKS CITED

Frederick Luis Aldama. 'Amitav Ghosh : *The Glass Palace*', *World Literature Today*. 75, ¾ Summer / Autumn, 2001.

Ghosh, Amitav. *The Glass Palace*, New Delhi: Harper Collins Publisher, 2001.

Trilling, Lionel. 1961. *The Liberal Imagination*, London: Mercury Books.

Ash, Timothy Garton, "Beauty and the Beast in Burma", *The New York Review of Books*, May 25, 2000, vol XL vii, No.9.

Desai, W.S., *A Pageant of Burmese History*, Orient Longman, 1961.

Ghosh, Amitav. *The Glass Palace*, Ravi Dayal Publisher, Delhi, 2000.

Hutchecon, Linda. *A Poetics of Postmodernism: History, Theory, Fiction*. Routledge, New York and London, 1988.

Jan Mohamad, Abdul, R., in *A Cultural Studies Reader: History, Theory, Practice*, ed. Jessica Munns and Gita Rajan. Longman Groups Ltd. 1995.

Kyi, Aung San Sui, *Burma and India: Some Aspects of Intellectual Life under Colonialism*, Allied Publisher, I.I.A.S. Shimla, 1990.

Trager, Frank, *Burma: From Kingdom to Republic: A Historical and Political Analysis*•, Pall Mall Press, London, 1966.

7

Conclusion

During the last two and half decades, a large number of novelists in Indian Fiction in English have attracted a great deal of attention and favourable comment. Famous among them are Kamla Markandaya, R. P. Jhabwala, Nayantara Sahgal, Veena Paintal, Attia Hussain, Jayshree Chatterjee, Nargis Dalal, Namita Gokhale, Tapti Mukherjee, Santha Rama Rao, Anita Desai and Amitav Ghosh.

Amitav Ghosh's engagement with some of the serious issues facing contemporary ex-colonies in Asia and Africa is reflected in his novels. Each one of his novels, whether it is *The Circle of Reason* [1986] or *The Shadow Lines* [1988], *In an Antique Land* [1993] or the recently published *The Glass Palace* [2000], is concerned with the impact of the colonial encounter on the political, social and cultural lives of the now independent countries, like, India, Bangladesh, Burma and Egypt. He is a writer of the shifting ongoing migrations and transnational cultural flows in different countries over different continents, a writer who questions the validities of boundaries and borders imposed by some powerful race / countries or communities over others. His writings explore and dissolve the boundaries of genres, disturbing the existing divisions of discourse into anthropology, history, fiction and autobiography.

The existential torment of modernist fiction is replaced in the post-colonial novel by a phenomenon one might: call 'existential anxiety'. Diaspora takes the place of doubt and homelessness becomes the principle trope, typifying a historical condition as well a state of mind. When Rushdie's narrator in *The Ground Beneath her Feet* dubs himself a 'photographer of exits' it is exactly this paradox to which he refers - of having to capture individuals and populations at the very moment that they are about to move *out* of a frame.

Colonialism had movement built into its definition: troops on the march, drastic changes in administration, large-scale transfers of goods and services and reconfigurations of political boundaries. Any writer who seeks to present the soul of man under colonialism, as Amitav Ghosh does in his latest novel, *The Glass Palace* is therefore con-demned to record the existential dilemma - wherein the subject is necessarily partitioned, a bewildered immigrant never quite in focus nor contained within the frame.

Ghosh's characters, in this most capacious of his fictions, literally include both kings [Thebaw, Queen Supalayat, the Burmese prin-cesses] and commoners [Dolly, Rajkumar, Saya John, Lima] but what unites them all is the inescapable narrative of colonial displacement. Buffeted about by the gale-winds of history, these protagonists are driven from Burma to India, Malaya, Singapore and back again, repeating each time a pattern of action that Ghosh presents in his first few pages:

As Ghosh tells us, 'a cloud of dust' tends to hang over the colonial scenario. Whole cities are on the run and it is often impossible to 'see far', given the panicky conditions. Under the circumstances, then, it is not surprising that Ghosh also uses, *A la* Rushdie, the metaphor of the camera to slow events down to a pace where it is actually possible to focus. The 'glass palace' of his title, it turns out, indicates both the magnificent hall of mirrors, which forms the centrepiece of the Mandalay residence of Burmese royalty *and* the name of a 'small photo studio' where the book's action appropriately ends.

The Circle of Reason [1986] is the most significant novel by Amitav Ghosh. It deals with the modern man's problem of alienation, migration and the existential crisis in life. Divided into three different section and called Satva: Reason, Rajas: Passion and Tamas: death, the novel symbolically deals with three phases of human life. Satva: symbolizes the search of wisdom, Rajas symbolizes the life of passion and Tamas stands for darkness, and destruction.

The Shadow Lines is a masterpiece in the contemporary Indo-English Literature. It leaves a lasting impression on the reader, with its structural intricacies and brilliance and thematic profundity. The main events of the novel take place in England, India and Pakistan during the turbulent times of war, communal riots and resulting ethos of uncertainty and inexplicable fear. Throughout the novel, the reader experiences a nagging threat of the forces of friction and destruction. The artificiality crated and politically maneuvered barriers between nation and nation, people and people, need to be transcended beyond the confines of time and space. Tridib's life and death bring out the tragic irony of the inescapable duality of the human mind. His spirit of Liberation is both triumph and a defeat, of his creative imagination and selfless love.

The novel no doubt tries to bring out the inner paradox of Tridib's life, and his efforts to overcome that. Tridib is a student of archaeology with deep interest in history. He can perceive not only 'the pastness of the past', but also live the pastness in the present. His 'imaginative eye' can see the permanent in the transient and explode all the artificial barriers of time and space. It escapes the bondage that limits ordinary human consciousness. He is the narrator's uncle by family relations. But a more profound emotional bond binds them. He is the narrator's 'idealized hero' and 'a mentor'. Tridib's search for the ideal world is kept alive by his nephew even after the former's death. Tridib's passionate dream of a completely integrated inner and outer world is expressed thus:

> "..... One could never knew anything except through desire, real desire ..... a pure, painful and primitive desire, a longing for everything that was not in one's self a torment of the flesh, that carried one beyond the limits of one's mind to another place and even, if one was lucky, to a place where there was no order between oneself and one's image in the mirror". [29]

This intense longing for 'everything that was not in oneself' and 'a place without any border' is almost like a hermit's speech for 'Adwait'. But paradoxically this passion for the ideal world is counter balanced in his real life by a detached and restrained attitude. He is introduced to the reader as 'a recluse' 'happiest in the neutral territory' of the strangers, 'most himself outside home' etc. Like Camus's 'Outsider', he is estranged and lonely. He does not submit to the narrow confines of time, place or person. He retains his freedom through creative inventions and the power of active imagination. He tells the narrator:

> ".... We could not see without inventing what we saw, so at least we could try to do it properly ... we had to try because the alternative wasn't blankness.... It only meant that if we didn't try ourselves, we would never be free of other people's inventions". [31]

There can be no inventions without imagination. But it is absolutely necessary to use it with 'precision', with great care and responsibility. The danger of succumbing to other people's invention is as threatening as the danger of 'improper imaginings', 'irresponsible inventing'. In order to gain and retain the real freedom, the mind has to first realize the true meaning of responsibility.

Fiction, at its best, provides us with 'addresses' for the lost actors in the historical chronicle. By dwelling on small details and bestowing on ordinary lives an attention that the historian's stricter annals cannot afford, a writer creates an *interior history*. Such an internalized record of emotions runs parallel to explicit factual accounts and fills them out.

At this elusive juncture, so to speak, story meets history and makes it a little more comprehensible. A genre like the novel, especially, is suited to the task of bringing content back to those empty frames from which the colonial subject is always vanishing. Like Ilongo, a novelist 'reaches into his pockets' and 'holds out' his 'smudged and crumpled sheet of paper' so that the reader can 'decipher' it in a manner that combines fact with affect, photographic accuracy with the uncertain-ties of memory. That is why I cannot think of a clutch of sentences, which better describe Ghosh's own labours in this massive 547-page book than these:

> "He has a small-photo studio. Does wedding-pictures, group photographs. That sort of thing.' It would be quite accurate to say that weddings and group portraits form the bulk of the matter in *The Glass Palace*".

Ghosh's technique is simply to borrow the war-journalist's tripod, lenses and so forth and then swivel his viewfinder so that it alights on families living out their lives in tumultuous times. It just happens that the subjects of his current book are Burmese citizens, but one can easily imagine Ghosh 'photographing' Afghan refugees or Kashmiri pundits using the same documentary method. Indeed, he has used the strategy with success in several previous works - dealing, for example, with the enigma of a divided Bengal in the *Shadow Lines* or establishing home-ly connections with a conventionally 'exotic' Egypt in *In an Antique Land*. To thus ground one's fiction in the genres of the traveller's tale, the anthropologist's notes, the historian's books, constitutes an almost unavoidable element of the postcolonial novel today - this very situ-ated-ness paradoxically attesting its travel-worthiness, as it were - an issue to which I return towards the end of this essay.

Postcolonial criticism has been called traveling theory, but the description applies equally, in my view, to the postcolonial novel. The very logic of its name seems to commit the postcolonial novel to reviewing the 'facts' presented through the lens of a colonial history by bringing them into the ambit of fiction. A certain mobility, an ability to shift perspectives and move between genres and cultures is thus implicit in that 'thou-shalt-not' injunction obeyed, in my view, by every significant sub-continental novelist writing in English today. Whether he knows it or not, [Ghosh clearly does, as evidenced by his vocal objections to being dubbed a 'Commonwealth writer' compelling for a 'Commonwealth Prize'], any 'major work' by such an author *cannot and may not* consist of private and a-historic acts of straight*forward* story-telling. That remains the privilege of those who write from a secure and unselfconsciously 'mainstream' Western perspect-ive. Among the writers who bear the label 'postcolonial', the right to be read 'world-wide' currently depends on a two-fold willingness - to retell the story of the colonizer-colonized relationship in a new, flexible 'multicultural' idiom and to 'travel Westwards' even as one 'stays East' in terms of subjects and themes.

However, critical and anti-imperialist their stances and however different their styles and temperaments, neither Salman Rushdie nor Allan Sealy nor Arundhati Roy nor Vikram Seth nor Amitav Ghosh could for one moment deny that they have embraced this ethical burden with considerable zest in their work. For the only way to make one's presence felt on a world-stage, be visible arid 'at home in the world', ironically, is to hark back, preferably in English, to a 'forgot-ten' history in which the colonizer participated as vigorously as the colonized.

At a international literary festival aptly entitled 'At Home in the World' held in Delhi in 2002 and attended by Ghosh, this point was reiterated in various ways, by both 'local' and 'diasporic' writers. The use of the erstwhile colonizer's tongue, English, for example, was itself regarded by some as incapable of capturing the 'authentic' flavour of 'the Indian experience'. Writing in English was seen as almost automatically rendering a writer elite, out-of-touch and emasculated almost a prototypical inhabitant of a removed ivory tower, or 'a glass palace", so to speak. Maybe those who lived in glass-houses were forbidden to throw stones,-but who said that they were guaranteed immunity from *being* pelted? That was the implicit message. Ghosh, however, seemed impatient with these gripes, dismissing the whole 'Indian languages versus English debate' as meaningless and *passe.* Not only did he read and admire contemporary writers in Bengali such as Mahasvveta Devi and Sunil Gangopadhyay, he was on excellent terms with them personally. A writer's business was to write and problematic values could, in his view, be interrogated as effectively through English as through any other 'Indian' language. So, he did not see where the problem lay! Speaking for himself, he confessed to me disarmingly, all he had ever wanted to do was *to* write and everything else arranged itself around this central and singular focus - language, place, profession, family, travel.

To this extent, the pivotal figure of Rajkumar in *The Glass Palace* now seems to me an in-text metaphor for Ghosh's own authorial persona, as he perceives himself. Like Ghosh, Rajkumar is a boundary-crosser, who makes several transitions across national frontiers during his life-time but he is also a man so absolutely focused that he *creates* his own destiny, his own history.

Ghosh's third book, *In an Antique Land* [1992], a text that straddles the generic borderlines between fact, fiction, autobiography, history, anthropology, and travel book. Ghosh maps ethnographic fieldwork undertaken in the Egyptian villages of Lataifa and Nashawy onto his subsequent research into medieval Indian Ocean trade. In so doing he explores the connections and ruptures between two worlds, the medieval and the contemporary. As the book progresses the two seemingly disparate strands of the Egyptian families and village communities with whom Ghosh resides in the early 1980s, and the narrative of his attempts to trace 'the slave of MS. H.6' increasingly dovetail, each narrative helping to shed light on the other.

Ghosh parodies and subverts the traditional ethnographic trope of confining personal commentary to prefaces or afterwards. He chooses to omit the conventional arrival scene, and his description of the Egyptian village begins with the narrator already settled, somewhat unhappily, at the house of Abu-'Ali. Whereas many classic ethnographies begin with an introduction describing the sense of strangeness felt by the ethnographer on arrival at the field site, and then banish personal observation from the main body of the text, Ghosh makes no mention of his arrival, though his feelings of alienation and the curiosity his presence provokes are emphasized throughout. Ghosh too sandwiches his text between a 'Prologue' and an 'Epilogue', but it is worth noting that these are more novelistic terms than the scholarly 'Preface' or 'Afterword', immediately indicating the text's imaginative purchase on anthropology.

Amitav Ghosh is one of the most popular names in the contemporary Indian English fiction writing. Whether it is *The Calcutta Chromosome* or *The Countdown* arrests the critical attention of the people in India as well as in abroad. *The Calcutta Chromosome* is a distinctive novel in the sense that it takes up the issue of Malaria and Mystery. In everyday life of India thousands of people die of this Malaria disease but it has been for the first time presented in the fictive form by the creative writer. The author in this novel deals with the subject of the malarial fever amalgamating it with mysticism and mystery, supernatural and superstition, considering it the philosophy of science and counter-science. The novelist argues:

> ".... Now Let's say jt here was something like Science and counter-science? Thinking of it in the abstract,

> wouldn't you say that the first principle of a functioning counter-science would have to be secrecy? The way I see it, wouldn't just have to be secretive about what it did [it couldn't hope to beat the scientists at the game anyway]; it would have to be secretive in what it did" [88].

Thematically Amitav Ghosh articulates secrecy, mystery and juxtaposes knowledge and comes across what he terms conventional knowledge. The central character of the novel, Murugan explains the intricacy of the subject matter. He says:

> "May be this other team started with the ideas that knowledge is self-contradictory, may be they believed that to know something is to change it, therefore, in knowing something, you've already changed what you think you know so you don't really know it at all: you only know its history. May be they thought mat knowledge couldn't begin without acknowledging the impossibility of knowledge" [88].

Murugan, the nucleus of the novel, a scientist has all command over the Malarial fever and the findings of Ronald Ross, a Nobel Laureate. He narrates the story to Antar, the Egyptian technocrat who too enjoys the company of Murugan in the same New York's Life - Watch with his computer AVA, The texture of the novel has been woven in a topsy-turvy manner which focuses the skilful effort of Murugan's play with the buttons on AVA. Everything happens like cinematography and Antar watches it like a film. Though everything is discussed in the twenty-first century but the scientific methodology of the discourse is altogether new one. The novel opens with the episode of the 21st century in Antar's flat in New York with the appearance of ID card on Ava's screen that demonstrates its system. This kind of computer has its own system for self-advancement. The novelist artistically displays this system of forthcoming era :

> "Anything she didn't recognize she'd take apart on screen, producing microscopic structural analyses, spinning the images around and around, tumbling them over, resting them on their side, producing ever greater refinements of details" [3-4].

Again he says

> "She had been programmed to hunt out real-time information, and that was what she was determined to get. Once she'd wrung the last, meaningless detail out of him, she'd give the object on her screen, final spin, with a bizarrely human smugness, before propelling, it into the horizonless limbo of her memory" [4].

This aforesaid statement purports the moods and moments of the novel and describes the panoramic details, which became apparent to Antar. It has been made clear by Murugan that the same events occurred earlier in 1995 in Calcutta and hundred years ago in Calcutta and Hyderabad. The novelist here makes a creative use of time through computer system in the same way as H.G. Wells does in "Time Machine" to move in time - past - present and future. From the reader's point of view it is the past of the 19th century, the contemporary time of August 1995 and the forthcoming time, which weave the centrality of the novel. The novelist has explored the philosophy of divided between narrated time and narrational time. Amitabh Ghosh tries to delve into the complexity of tint theory, which can be understood by the English theoreticians.

The Calcutta Chromosome is a befitting example of this classification made by Berdyaev. Whatever way time is classified, as conceptual or perceptual as choronos or kairos, its paramount significance to the creative writer and his art is unavoidable. Vance Bourjaily rightly pinpoints that "the structure of the novel comes from how you decide to handle time." In fact, time leads to certain developments in a causal sequence, culminating in a particular result: What is stressed here is that events unfold in a causal order and one thing leads to another. The novelist wittingly shuffles time in such a way that a reader often loses track of all time references. There is a dialectical relationship between clock time and psychological time with no before and after connections. *The Calcutta Chromosome* is a novel in which poly temporal time - scheme has been employed. In the poly temporal time-schemes there is a constant shift from past to present to future. Connections of time and space are displaced by a more fundamental search for axiological connections. A value becomes extra-temporal and clock -time is subjugated to the inner experience of time.

Antar after the sincere speculation of two hours over Murugan's studies and experience of two days in Calcutta of the 19th century comes to unfold the hidden mystery of the events. The perusal of the text crystallizes this fact that the story has been conceived at three levels of time through AVA. Theologically the novelist peeps into the oriental philosophy of religion, birth and rebirth, transposition and transcendence that is very akin to dramatic satisfaction. In the light of scientific discovery of Ronald Ross the novelist depicts the supernatural power of Mangala, secretary to D.D, Cunningham. She is considered to be a goddess incarnate - who suggests a cure for syphilis. She too has the potency of transcending life beyond life. The contextual analysis of the letter of Parley conveys the two interesting parallel events in relation to Mangala in 1893. Parley being a scientist does not believe in rituals performed by Mangala so he warns the common people and exposes the false belief of the lady. Simultaneously he watches the development very curiously. Later he switches over to his own job to see 'the transformations that Laveran described'. He studies the slides smeared with the dying pigeon's blood. Then,

"he say Laveran's rods appear, hundreds of them,

> tiny cylindrical things, with their pointed penetrating heads piercing the blood miasma" [128].

In fact, new invention was made by his teammates exclusively meant for the future time. Parley's knowledge about Mangala brought his doom. He is promised by Mangala through the young boy assistant to reveal everything. "If I would but accompany him to his birth place, fortunately the place of which he spoke is not far from the location of my clinic. We are to leave tomorrow' [129]. Elijah Parley did not reach to his destination, he disappeared in the midst of his journey; never appeared again. It has been discovered by the police that he had indeed boarded the train at Sealdah, as scheduled but had disappeared before his destination - a remote rarely used station called Renupur, m severe monsoon weather. Later it was reported that a young man had been seen carrying his luggage. It has been said that his knowledge for Mangala proved to be fatal for him. The letter, which has been written by Parley, seems to be instrumental for Murugan in constructing the plot of encounter between Farley and Mangala and the disappearance of Parley. Now, there remains nothing about Parley's knowledge and the existence of that letter. The author creates mystery about Parley's intelligence and his disappearance. In the same manner, another incident takes place in 1995. Once Sonali comes out to locate the whereabouts of Roman Haldar at Robinson Street. The novelist says -

> "She caught a glimpse of tops of dozens of heads, some male, some female, young and old, packed in close together. Their faces were obscured by the obscured by the smoke and flickering firelight." [139]

Roman Haldar's and Mrs. Arafounian's bodies are set for the ritual performance. Romen Haldar decides to meet Sonali during evening hour but all on a sudden he disappears. According to the design of the novel, the novelist does not think necessary to explore his sudden demise or what he calls, disappearance. Both the events occur at the difference of hundred years accentuates the intricacy and mystification of the plot. In case of Parley his knowledge has been kept unknown which is proved to be decisive in his disappearance - death. Even in relation to Haldar nothing has been chalked out barring the incident of mysterious rituals, which are, performed the Calcutta in 1995 in the name of some special knowledge of transcendence. Afterwards, the novelist again weaves a story of a stationmaster who is murdered at Renupur, [the place where Parley disappeared in 1894] on a moonless night by Laakhan. In the year of 1933, Phulboni fortunately saves himself from the train accident. Same is the case in 1895 when Grigson had hardly saved himself. Both the incidents took place in the same circumstances and the persons who were trying to kill them were not recognized. Phulboni himself narrates Laakhan, the ghost trains, which he visualised, and also the ghost-station master with whom he encounters. In the heart of the novel Lutchman, Laakha, Lucky of the 19th, the 20th and the 21st centuries appear and disappear. As a matter of fact, these characters are not even constructed or projected as multi-faced characters. Stylistically, the organization of the novel is something unique. Murugan correlates the same boy who once comes at the doorstep of Urmila with fish wrapped in papers as Laakhan. The novelist finds a common feature in connection with all these boys that they have a deformed thumb. The novel after all does not ensure any physical or intellectual improvisation.

Owing to these parallel developments of the plot, the mystery of the novel gradually becomes acute and intense. No body can say convincingly as to which direction the novel is moving ahead. In all the mystery novels the novelists make a successful attempt to arrive at the resolution. At last the Ava presents Murugan, Urmila and Sonali going towards the station Sealdah, where they came to know that Phulbone and Mrs. Arnouin have left the venue. Murugan too have been found. Later, missing from here. Everything has been left to the imagination of the

·eader. This is Sealdah Station from where everyone has been disappearing. At the moment they are going towards the station in 1995 while Urmila utters that she would protect them and take them across and the next moment, Antar listening sounds, getting similarity between Tara and Urmila and Maria and Sonali, speaking to him, as if they were accompanying him in his room,

> "a voice whispering in his ear, 'keep watching' we are here, we are all with you" [256].

There are so many queries and questions, which lurk in the void. No body argues from what he is to be saved and where he has to go across. The novelist explains everything in the galaxy of his theory of counter-science and secrecy and contradictions of knowledge. He himself points out "what I'm really talking about is technology for inter - personal transference" [90]. This technology is considered to be *The Calcutta Chromosome.* Herein we find the echoes of the *Bhagvad Gita,* about body being a sort of garment to be discarded when it turns old and torn to acquire a new, fresh garment for the soul. The end result of the application of this theory to the characters in the novel is far from satisfactory. Amitav Ghosh in his unconvincing attempt scrutinizes the topical issue of the recurrence of the malarial fever and the theory of time and space. The Edwardian novel was felt to neglect psychological for physical detail and to run in the current of time and space without diving deep into the infinite potentiality of any one moment. Whatever is most valuable in modem/post modem fiction writing is a meditation on the nature of time, on the mystery of memory and personality. The meeting of the past and present defining differences as well as similarities is crucial to the novel. The narrative moves up and down through layers of time. The whole pattern is a marriage of past and present with the flying multiplicity of the future racing towards one.

In a nutshell, Amitav Ghosh is considered to be one of the burgeon-ing groups of Post-Rushdie Indian novelists in English for whom globalization is an everyday fact of existence. Like such novelists as Rushdie, Seth, Desai and Mistry, Ghosh seems to move effortlessly across national frontiers - as Robert Dixon puts it, not inhabiting -

"a culture rooted in a single place, but a discursive space that flows across political and national boundaries, and even across genera-tions in time". [1996: 9]

Dixon's remark refers specifically to Ghosh's second novel, *The Shadow Lines* [1988], which takes the events that followed in the wake of Partition as its central subject, suggesting that the carto-graphical shadow-lines that divide Bengal are political fictions that nonetheless generate all-too-real murderous consequences. 'Shadow lines' are, however, far more than just the borders constructed by politicians. They are also the lines of demar-cation that separate colonized and colonizer, present and past, self and image. Ultimately they are the signifying acts that construct notions of discrete identity [1996: 95-96]. Ghosh projects a view in which the frontier that separates India from East Pakistan / Bangladesh is a 'looking-glass border' [*The Shadow Lines:* 228] and in which complex affinities link the apparently dichotomized worlds of colonizer and colonized.

WORKS CITED

Bourjaely, Vance. A certain kind of work *In Afterwards* ed. Thomas McCormack, quoted in Higdon, p. 3.

Jameson, Frederick. *Marxism and Form,* New Jersey, 1971, p. 117.

Bhatt, Indira. Disappearances and Discovery a study of Amitabh Ghosh's *The Calcutta Chromosome* in 50 *Years of Indian Writing,* ed. by R.K. Dhawan, IAES, New Delhi, 1999, p. 49.

Robert Dixon, ' "Travelling in the West": The Writing of Amitav Ghosh', *The Journal of Commonwealth Literature,* 31.1, 1996, 9.

John Thieme. 'Passages to England', *Liminal Postmodernism!: The Postmodern, the [Post-]Colonial and the [Post-] Feminist*, ed. Theo D'haen and Hans Bertens, Amsterdam and Atlanta: Rodopi, 1994, pp. 65-66.

Ghosh, Amitav. 1986, *The Circle of Reason*, London: Himash Hamilton.

______. 1988, *The Shadow Lines*, New Delhi: Ravi Dayal Publisher.

______. 1992, *In An Antique Land*, New Delhi: Ravi Dayal Publisher.

______. 1966, *The Calcutta Chromosome*, New Delhi: Ravi Dayal Publisher.

______. 1998, *Dancing in Cambodia, At Large in Burma*, New Delhi: Ravi Dayal Publisher.

______. 1999, *Countdown*, New Delhi: Ravi Dayal Publisher.

______. 2000, *The Glass Palace*, New Delhi: Ravi Dayal Publisher and Permanent Black.

Bibliography

Primary Sources

Ghosh, Amitav. 1986, *The Circle of Reason*, London: Himash Hamilton.

______. 1988, *The Shadow Lines*, New Delhi: Ravi Dayal Publisher.

______. 1992, *In An Antique Land*, New Delhi: Ravi Dayal Publisher.

______. 1966, *The Calcutta Chromosome*, New Delhi: Ravi Dayal Publisher.

______. 1998, *Dancing in Cambodia, At Large in Burma*, New Delhi: Ravi Dayal Publisher.

______. 1999, *Countdown*, New Delhi: Ravi Dayal Publisher.

______. 2000, *The Glass Palace*, New Delhi: Ravi Dayal Publisher and Permanent Black.

Secondary Sources

A. Books on and about Amitav Ghosh

Asnani, Shyam. *New Dimensions of Indian English Novel*, Delhi: Doaba House, 1987.

Beach, J. W. 1965, *Twentieth Century Novel*. India: Lyall Book Depot.

Bhargava, Rajul [ed.]. 2002, *Indian Writing in English: The Last Decade.* Jaipur and New Delhi : Rawat Publications.

Bhatt, Indira and Indira Nityanandam. *The Fiction of Amitav Ghosh,* New Delhi: Creative Books, 2001.

Bhatnagar, Manmohan [ed.]. 1996, *Twentieth Century Literature in English, Vol. I , II & III.* New Delhi: Atlantic Publishers and Distributors.

Bhatnagar, M. K. and M. Rajeshwar. 1999, Post-Modernism and English *Literature.* New Delhi: Atlantic Publishers and Distributors.

Barat, Urbashi, "Imagination and Reality" in *The Shadow Lines.* Delhi: Prestige Books, 1999.

Blackstone, Bernard. *Amitav Ghosh – A Commentary,* London, 1999.

Buchen, Irvin H. '*The Aesthetics of the Supra-novel* in John Halperin's [ed] *The Theory of Novel,* New York: Oxford University Press, 1974.

Burgess, Anthony. 1971, *The Novel Now.* London: Faber.

Chowdhary, Arvind [ed.]. 2002, *Amitav Ghosh's* The Shadow Lines. New Delhi: Atlantic Publishers and Distributors.

Cook, David, *African Literature : A Critical View,* London: Orient Longman, 1977.

Devy, G. N. *In Another Tongue,* Chennai: Macmillan, 1995.

Diaches, David. *Amitav Ghosh.* London: Oxford University Press, 1988.

Das, Bhagwan. 1985, *The Laws of Manu.* Vol. 1, Delhi: Aparna Publications.

Das, R. M. 1993, *Women in Manu's Philosophy.* Jalandhar: ABS Publications.

Das, S. 1929, *Purdah – the Status of Indian Women.* New Delhi: Ess Publications.

Deheja, Vidya. Ed. 1997, *Representing the Body: Gender Issues in Indian Art.* New Delhi: Kali for Women.

Ghadhially, Rehana. 1988, *Women in Indian Society*. New Delhi: Sage Publications.

Harrex, S. C. 1971, *The Fire and the Offering: English Language and Novel of India*. Calcutta: Writers Workshop.

Jain, Jasbir. 1998, *Women's Writing, Text and Context*. Jaipur and New Delhi: Rawat Publications.

Jain, Pratibha and Mohan, Rajan. 1996, Ed. *Woman Images*. New Delhi: Rawat Publications.

Kaul, A. N. *A Reading of The Shadow Lines*, from Amitav Ghosh's *The Shadow Lines*, Delhi: OUP, 1995.

Kaul, Suvir. "Separation Anxiety : Growing Up Inter/ National in *The Shadow Lines*. In Ghosh 268-286.

Khan, Fawzia, Afzal. 1993, *Cultural Imperialism and the Indo-English Novel*. Pennsylvania: Pennsylvania University Press.

Kirpal, Viney. Ed. *The New Indian Novel in English*, Delhi: Allied Publishers Pvt. Ltd., 1990.

Lal, Malashree. 1995, *The Law of the Threshold: Women Writers in Indian English*. Indian Institute of Advanced Study, Rashtrapati Nivas, Shimla.

Latham, J. E. M. [ed.] 1970, *Critics on Amitav Ghosh*, Florida.

Parameswaran, Uma. *A Study of Representative Indo-English Novelists*, New Delhi: Vikas, 1976.

Pynchon, Thomas. *The Crying of Lot 49*, Philadelphia : J. B. Lippincott, 1966.

Rajan, Rajeshwari. *The Division of Experience in The Shadow Lines*, from Amitav Ghosh's *The Shadow Lines*, Delhi: OUP, 1995.

Rao, Damodar K. 'Magic and Irony as Principles of Structure : A Reading of *The Circle of Reason*', in R. K. Dhawan's *The Novels of Amitav Ghosh*, New Delhi: Prestige Books, 1999.

Roy, Virendra K.1999, *Landmarks in Modern English Literature : Critical Appreciation of Life and Literary Values*. New Delhi: Kanishka Publishers and Distributors.

Tharu, Susie and K. Lalita. 1995, *Women Writing in India.* Vol. I and Vol. II. Delhi: Oxford University Press.

Tiwari, Shubha. 2003. *Amitav Ghosh : A Critical Study,* New Delhi: Atlantic Publishers and Distributors.

Trilling, Lionel. 1961. *The Liberal Imagination,* London: Mercury Books.

Walsh, William. 1973. [ed.], *Reading in Commonwealth,* London: Oxford University Press.

B. Articles

Ahmad, Aijaz. 'Post-Colonial Theory and the 'Post'-Condition'. Talk delivered at the Punjabi University, Patiala in May, 1997, pp. 1-40.

Atma, Ram, 'An Interview with Anita Desai,' *World Literature Written in English, XVI : I* [April 1977], p. 97.

Bhatt, Indira. 'Disappearances and Discovery a study of Amitav Ghosh's *The Calcutta Chromosome*' in *50 Years of Indian Writing*, ed. by R.K. Dhawan, IAES, New Delhi, 1999.

Bourjaely, Vance, 'A certain kind of work In *Afterwards*' ed. Thomas McCormack, quoted in Higdon.

Dewett, M. E. 'Why Writer in English?' *Times Literary Supplement,* 10 August 1962.

Dixon, Rovert. "Travelling in the West: The Writing of Amitav Ghosh", *The Journal of Commonwealth Literature,* 31.1,1996.

Guha, Sharmila. '*The Shadow Lines* and *In An Antique Land*', London, 1996.

Jameson, Frederick. *Marxism and Form,* New Jersey, 1971.

Joshi, Sudhakar. 'An Evening with Bhabani', *The Sunday Standard,* 27 April, 1969.

______.*The Journal of Indian Writing in English,* Vol. 9, No. 1, Ed. G. S. Balarama Gupta, Annamalai University, Jan. 1981.

______. 'Interview with Anita Desai', World Literature Written in English', Arlington, 16, April I, 1977.

Karnad, Girish. *'Worlds within Worlds'*, Book Review of *The Shadow Lines*, Indian Express Magazine, 18 Dec. 1988.

Malgaonkar, Manohar. 'Purdah and Castemarks', *The Times Literary Supplement*, 4 June, 1964.

Menon, Ritu and Kamla Bhasin, 'Recovery, Rupture, Resistance: Indian State and Abduction of Women During Partition,' in *Economic and Political Weekly*, 28, no. 17 [April 24, 1993].

Mukherjee, Meenakshi, 'Review in India Today', May 15,1996.

Ravi Nanda Sinha, 'Alienation in Indian Novel in English', *The Quest* [The Journal of Indian Literature and Culture], L. Manjula Davidson.

_____. 'Self / Other Binary Opposition in Anita Desai's *Bye-Bye, Blackbird, The Quest* [The Journal of Indian Literature and Culture], V-19, No.1, June 2005, Sharad Srivastava.

P. Vijay Kumar, 'Identity Crisis: Indian English Novelist in a Globalized World', *Litcrit,* an Indian Response to Literature, 59, V.31, No. 1, June 2005.

'Book I Enjoyed Writing Most', *Contemporary Indian Literature,* Vol. 13, No. 4, Oct. -Dec.1973, pp. 23-24.

'Book Review of *Hymns in Darkness*. *THE IPEN*, March-April, 1977, No. 3-4.

'Calcutta Kaleidoscope' *The Illustrated Weekly of India,* 1958.

'Contemporary English Literature in India' *Litcrit* (8), Jan. 1982, pp. 65-68.

'Flight of Forms', *Indian International Center Quarterly,* Vol. 10, No. 4, 1983, pp. 409.

'Gangtok', London: *Envoy,* 1959.

'Literary Lapses', *Book Review,* Vol, VII, No. 1, July/August 1982, pp. 8-10.

'Memoirs of Mendicant Professor: *A Review*', *The Quest,* 66, July-Sept., 1970.

'The Indian Writer's Problems', *The Literary Criterion,* Vol. XI, No. 4, Autumn, 1975, pp. 29-32.

'The Timid Movement of a Wing', *The Indian Literary Review,* Aug. 1978.

'Within and Without Tradition', ACALLAS News Letter, Mysore-5, April, 1979, pp. 5-21.

'Women Writers', *Quest,* No. 65, April-June, 1970, pp. 39-40.

Paranjape, Makarand. 'Inside and Outside the Whale: Politics and the New Indian English Novel', ed. Viney Kirpal, *The New Indian Novel in English,* Delhi: Allied Publishers Pvt. Ltd., 1996.

Rao, C. V. 'Woman and Fiction', *The Literary Criterion,* VII, 3, Winter 1966, p. 48.

Rao, Maithili. 'Landscape of the Mind', *Eve's Weekly,* 6 August, 1983, pp. 52-55.

Ram, Atma. 'Indians Slow to Recognize Talent in Their Midst', *The Tribune,* 26 June, 1977.

Singh, Khushwant. 'Address to Expo 1967 Auditorium Montreal, Canada, 1967.

Taneja, G. R. 'The Novel Today', *World Literature Today,* University of Oklahama, Spring, 1991.

C. Webliography

www.ajax prenhall.com. http://www.ajax.prenhall.com

www.anothersucontinent.com.http://www.anothersubcontinent.com/forums/index.php?showtopic=1868

www.answers.com.http://www.answers.com/main/ntquery?method=4&dsname=Wikipedia+Images&dekey=Anita_Desai.jpg&gwp=8

www.new.bbc.co.uk.http://new.bbc.co.uk/2/hi/entertainment/6745609.stm.

www.worldcat.org/http://worldcat.org/issn/0315-4149.

www.sunnewsonline.com/http://sunnewsonline.com/webpages/features/literari/2006/oct/01/literari-01-10-2006-001.html.

www.time.com/time/2005/100books/the _complete-list.html.

www.geogianencyclopedia.org.http://www.georgianencyclopedia.org/nge/Article.jsp?id=h-2895.

www.schweitzwe.org.http://www.schweitzwe.org/english/aseind.html.

www.iblict.com/http://iblict.com/author611.html.

Index